LONGMAN LITERAT

Twisters

Stories before 1900

Editor: Erik Wilcock

 LONGMAN

Other titles in the Longman Literature series are listed on pages 164 and 165.

Contents

CONTENTS

Introduction

The main idea behind this collection was to assemble some short stories which were written before 1900, because this is an important part of the National Curriculum in English.

The nice thing about these stories is that they are short but have a lot to say. They also have a twist in the tale, which is why the collection is called *Twisters*. Another consideration was to include stories from around the world. Races and cultures may have their differences but one thing is certain: they all tell stories. It seems to be an important way of making sense of the world we live in.

As you will notice, many of the stories do not have authors. They are classed as folk tales or 'traditional'. This means that they are stories which have been going around for a long time. They were probably not written down to begin with and were just handed on from generation to generation. That is probably the best compliment the stories could receive: people just wanted to hear and to tell them again and again.

The stories in this collection have been grouped together under headings. This has been done to help you think about the similarities and the differences between each story. At the end of the selection you will also see a variety of assignments giving you opportunities to write about and discuss the stories.

▉ The collection

Classic fairy tales

- **'The Tinderbox' by Hans Christian Andersen**
  Danish; written around 1850, translation 1990

  Hans Christian Andersen (1805–1875) was born in Odense. His father was a cobbler. He is considered to be one of the finest writers of fairy tales and many of his famous stories, like '**The Snow Queen**', '**The Emperor's New Clothes**' and '**The Red Shoes**' are highly original. The stories were not just written for children; they contain powerful messages for all age ranges. Andersen travelled widely and became friends with Charles Dickens, who was a great admirer of his work.

- **'The Magic Ring'**
  Middle Eastern; traditional

Winners

- **'The Creation of Man'**
  American Indian myth

- **'From Tiger to Anansi'**
  Caribbean folk tale

Norwegian stories – death by drowning

- ## 'The Father' by Björnstjerne Björnson
  written 1895; translation 1996

  Börnstjerne Björnson (1832–1910) won the Nobel Prize for Literature in 1903. He is one of Norway's major writers and was most active at the same time as Henrik Ibsen. He was director of the National Theatre in Bergen and had a great interest in drama, writing many plays that were popular at the time. He was proud of his country and his writing about its past, its myths and legends helped the movement which finally made Norway an independent nation again in 1905.

- ## 'The Fisherman' by Jonas Lie
  written 1890; translation 1996

  Lack of money and job prospects drove Jonas Lie (1833–1909) to try his hand at writing. Although he wrote three excellent novels which focused their attention on the struggles of family life, he is probably best known for his collection of short stories called *Trold*. These stories, like '**The Fisherman**' ('Isak og Bronnoypresten'), manage to blend real life with fantastic and haunting events to great effect.

Losers

- **'The Pardoner's Tale' by Geoffrey Chaucer**
  (1) 1990 translation; (2) original version written
  around 1380

  Geoffrey Chaucer (1343–1400) is called by many the
  father of English literature. His most famous work,
  The Canterbury Tales, was a mammoth project. He
  devised a huge storytelling competition: twenty-nine
  people are making their way to Canterbury
  Cathedral from the Tabard pub in London. The
  landlord, Harry Bailly, suggests that these pilgrims
  should each tell four stories – two on the way to
  Canterbury and two on the way back – to make
  their journey more interesting (116 tales in all); the
  winner is to receive a slap-up meal at his pub.
  Chaucer managed to complete only twenty-one of
  these tales before his death; '**The Pardoner's Tale**'
  is one.

  Chaucer lived a varied life. He was linked to the
  royal court and served it in different ways. At one
  point he was in charge of Customs; he was later a
  Justice of the Peace and also Member of Parliament.
  He travelled widely in Europe and was extremely
  well read.

- **'The Monkey's Paw' by W. W. Jacobs**
  written 1898

  William Wymark Jacobs (1863–1943) was born in
  Wapping. His father worked on the local docks. He

was a clerk to begin with, but the success of his short stories led him to give up his job to become a full-time writer. Although many of his stories are humorous and deal with seafaring folk, it is his dark and macabre stories which proved to be best-sellers.

Relationships

- ### 'A New England Nun' by Mary Wilkins Freeman
  American; written 1898

  Mary Wilkins Freeman (1852–1930) was born in Massachusetts. She wrote mainly about New England and was first and foremost a short-story writer. Her work was extremely popular during her lifetime.

- ### 'The Necklace' by Guy de Maupassant
  French; written 1885, translation 1990

  Guy de Maupassant (1850–93) is considered by many to be one of the finest writers of short stories. His attention to small detail makes his work very accessible. Maupassant wrote about ordinary people but his stories have unusual twists and turns.

- ### 'The Gift of the Magi' by O. Henry
  American; written 1899

  O. Henry (1862–1910), whose real name was William Sydney Porter, was famous for his stories with a twist in the tale: the phrase 'an O. Henry ending' became quite well known. O. Henry began his writing career in jail. He was imprisoned for embezzling money and took to writing in his cell. Many believe that he got a great deal of the material for his stories from his fellow prisoners. Like Maupassant, O. Henry dealt with ordinary people. He revealed their lives to his readers in a way they understood, and then hit them with his famous 'O. Henry ending'.

Reading step by step

In this section there is one short assignment to help you make more sense of each story.

1   The Tinderbox

The soldier in the story is meant to be the hero. As you read, think closely about his actions towards others – are they good, are they bad?

2   The Magic Ring

Like '**The Tinderbox**', this is also a fairy tale. As you read, note down some of the ingredients which go into making a classic fairy tale.

3   The Creation of Man

This is an American Indian version of Man's creation. What ideas do you get about the different types of animals in this story? Do they remind you of humans at all?

4 From Tiger to Anansi

Usually people are not keen on spiders, yet Anansi is regarded as something of a hero in Caribbean countries. What is there to admire about Anansi?

5 David and Goliath

What similarities do you notice between this story and the previous story?

6 The Conceited Man

Compare the actions of Li Chao with those of the girl he challenges at the end of the story.

7 The Selfish Giant

Look at the opening section of the story. How does Oscar Wilde make everything appear to be dark and without love?

8 Tseng and the Holy Man

At one point in the story, Tseng has a dream. How realistic do you think this section of the story is?

9   Gypsies Who All But Cheated Themselves

This story has many twists and turns. Make a note of each time the story has a twist in it and look in detail at the way it affects the two central characters.

10   The Gypsy Who Did Not Keep His Word

Look at the actions of the central character. As you do so, think about the way the two characters behaved in the previous story. Why do you think that this character comes to a bad end, whereas the two in '**The Fisherman**' do not?

11   The Father

During his interviews with Tor, the vicar asks if there is anything else Tor wishes to say or add to their conversation. What do you think he is giving Tor the chance to say or do?

12   The Fisherman

In the previous story the problems lay with the central character, Tor. In this story the problems lie more with the vicar. Look at the way he reacts to Isak's requests. Do you think he acts reasonably?

13 The Pardoner's Tale

When the character of the old man appears, think about who he might be. Draw a sketch of him.

14 The Monkey's Paw

As you read through the story, make notes on what you think the Whites do wrong. When you have finished the story, ask yourself whether they deserve what happens to them?

15 A New England Nun

Draw up two columns: one headed 'Reasons for marrying Joe', the other headed 'Reasons against'. As you read, think about what Louisa would lose if she married Joe and what she would gain.

16 The Necklace

Draw a bar chart to show the changing fortunes of Madame Loisel. Write 'Bad fortune' at the bottom of the vertical axis and 'Good fortune' at the top. Make a list of the events which affect her fortune, set them along the horizontal axis and produce a bar for each.

17 The Gift of the Magi

What do you think of the character of Della? Do you think she makes the right choice in deciding to raise twenty dollars for a Christmas present?

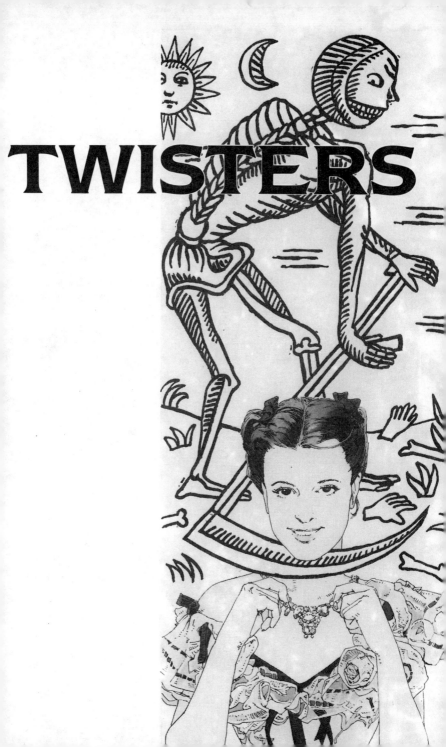

TWISTERS

The Tinderbox

U P-TWO-THREE FOUR. Up-two-three... A soldier came marching down the road. He had a knapsack on his back and a sword by his side, for he had been to war and now he was going home. Suddenly he came across an old witch standing in the middle of the road; she was so ugly: her lower lip dangled down over her chest. 'Good evening, Mr Soldier,' she said, 'What an excellent sword you have by your side; and what a hefty knapsack. Now you are what I call a real soldier! Come closer, Mr Soldier. Listen, if you want to, you can have more money than you ever dreamed of.'

'Well, thank you very much, old witch. But what do I have to do?'

'You see this big tree, here,' she said pointing to a great oak. 'It's completely hollow inside. Now, if you clamber up to the top of it, you'll find a hole there. That's the way in – slide down carefully and you'll be right in the heart of the tree.'

'What on earth am I supposed to do in the heart of an oak tree?' asked the soldier.

'Get the money, of course. You see, when you're there you'll see a huge passageway lit by a hundred burning torches and right ahead of you are three doors – and you can open them, because the keys are in the locks. If you go into the first room, you will see a large chest with a dog sitting on top of it. This dog has eyes as big as tea cups. But don't bother yourself about that: I will give you my blue-checked apron to deal with him. All you do is spread the apron on the floor, grab hold of the dog and put him on it. You can now open up the chest and take out as much money as you like. Of course, the coins in this chest are all copper, so if you'd prefer silver you'll have to go into the next room. The dog in this room has eyes as big as millstones, but don't worry your self about that. Just put him on the apron and take the money. Now, if it's gold you're after, there's tons of that too, but it's in the third room. The dog in this room is what I call a real dog. His eyes are as big as the Round Tower in Copenhagen but don't bother yourself about old big eyes! Just stick him on the apron like you did with the other two and he won't touch you. Then you'll be able to take as much gold as you can carry.'

'Sounds like a good idea to me,' said the soldier, 'but what's in it for you, old hag? What's the catch?'

'I don't want any money,' replied the witch, 'All I ask is that you fetch a tinderbox that my old granny left behind the last time she was in the tree.'

'OK, then. Tie the rope around my waist.'

'Right – that's done. And you'll be needing this,' said the witch, handing him the blue-checked apron.

So the soldier gingerly climbed to the top of the tree. Once there, he slid into the heart of the oak where he discovered the huge passageway flanked by a hundred burning torches.

He went to the first door and opened it. Oh! There indeed was the dog with eyes as big as tea cups; and it sat and stared directly at him.

'You're a bonny chap,' said the soldier as he removed the dog from the chest and popped him on the witch's apron. Then he crammed his pockets full of copper coins, shut the chest and put the watchdog back on top of it.

He went into the second room. My goodness! There it was: the dog with eyes as big as millstones. 'Don't look at me like that,' said the soldier. 'You'll strain your eyes!' And with that he grabbed the dog and popped him on the witch's apron. When he saw all the silver coins, he threw away the copper ones and crammed his pockets full of shining silver – then he opened his knapsack and filled it to the brim with coins as well.

Next he stepped inside the third room. What a revolting sight! It was just as the witch had said: the dog did have eyes as big as the Round Tower but, worse still, they spun round in his head like huge wheels.

'Good evening,' said the soldier, as he approached the dog. He didn't know what else to say. After all he had never seen anything like it. But, after giving the dog the once over, he made up his mind. He grabbed hold of it and swiftly popped it down on the witch's apron. And so to the third chest – you would not believe how much

3

gold there actually was in there. You could buy the whole of Copenhagen with that and still have change to buy all the sugar mice, tin soldiers, riding whips and rocking horses in the whole wide world. What a hoard!

The soldier ditched all the silver coins now, emptied his knapsack, and started loading himself up with gold. He filled his pockets, his knapsack, his hat – he even filled his boots; he could hardly walk. What did it matter, though? He was rich, rich, rich.

He slammed the door behind him, having first replaced the dog on the chest. Then he shouted up to the witch, 'Pull me up, old witch.'

'Have you got the tinderbox?' came the reply.

'That's a point,' said the soldier, 'I'd forgotten all about that.' And he went back to fetch it. Then the witch hauled him up and in no time he was back on the road again with his pockets, boots, knapsack and hat chock full of gold.

'Tell me – what do you want the tinderbox for?'

'None of your business,' said the witch. 'You've got your money, now hand over the tinderbox.'

'Naughty, naughty,' said the soldier. 'If you don't tell me why you want the tinderbox, I shall be forced to cut your head off.'

'Never!' screeched the witch.

So the soldier chopped her head off.

The soldier took her blue-checked apron and bundled the gold in it so that he could carry it over his shoulder. Then he slipped the tinderbox into his pocket and set off towards the town.

It was such a picturesque town and he made sure that he put up at the most luxurious inn. He ordered the best rooms and the choicest food: for now he was a rich man, with money coming out of his ears.

The servant who polished the boots couldn't help thinking it strange that the soldier's boots were so worn-out. The soldier told him that he hadn't had time to buy any. Next day, however, he went out and bought himself a complete outfit (the finest money could buy). It wasn't long before he became well-known as a refined young gentleman.

Everywhere he went all he ever heard about was the King and the fact that he had a very beautiful daughter.

'How could I get a look at her?' asked the soldier.

'You can't,' was the reply. 'She lives in the massive Copper Castle, surrounded by thick walls and high towers. The King is very careful who goes in there because it has been foretold that she will marry a common soldier; and he cannot bear the prospect of that happening.'

'What I wouldn't give to get a look at her,' mused the soldier, knowing full well that the chances of that happening were very remote indeed.

What a life he lived now: he went to the theatre, rode out in the Palace Gardens and made a point of giving lots of money to the poor because he remembered only too well what it was like to be down-and-out. He really was well-off now – he had beautiful clothes and lots of friends who thought he was the tops; a real cavalier, they called him. And he could put up with that, make no mistake.

The trouble was that as the cash flowed out, nothing came back in; and soon he was down to his last two gold coins. He had to leave his luxurious apartment and move into a small attic room. He had to clean his own boots and do his own darning. His friends stopped visiting; there were too many steps to climb to the new lodgings.

One dismal evening as the soldier sat in the dark and cold, he suddenly remembered that there was a candle stub in the old tinderbox that he got from the hollow tree. So he found the tinderbox, took out the bit of old candle and struck the flint. At that very moment the door flew open and there was the dog with eyes as big as tea cups, the very one he had seen in the tree. There it stood and it began to open its mouth, 'What is my master's command?'

'Goodness me,' said the soldier. 'This is some tinderbox if it can make wishes come true. Listen, bring me some money.'

No sooner had he said this, than the dog vanished. Within seconds it was back with a large bag of coins in its jaws. Now it began to dawn on the soldier how magical the tinderbox really was. Strike it once and along came the copper-coin dog, twice the silver and strike three times and there was gold, gold, gold.

The soldier moved back to his luxurious apartment, got another complete set of new clothes and was soon the centre of attention again; his friends thought so much of him now, you see.

One day the soldier sat pondering about the Princess. It seemed criminal that no one could see her. She was supposed to be so beautiful, everyone agreed. But what was the point of all that beauty if she was locked up inside the Copper Castle? 'So I can't see her, eh? Where's my tinderbox?' He struck the flint and the dog with eyes as big as tea cups appeared.

'I know it's the middle of the night but I would dearly like to see the Princess. You know, just a glimpse.' Off went the dog and, before the soldier could count to ten, returned with the princess. She lay on the dog's back fast asleep; and indeed she was beautiful. Any fool could have seen she was a real Princess. The soldier could not help himself: he had to kiss her – well, he was a real soldier, after all! Then the dog took the Princess back again.

Next morning while the King and Queen were sipping their tea, the Princess remarked that she had had a strange dream about a dog and a soldier: she had ridden on the dog's back and the soldier had kissed her. 'What a quaint little story,' said the Queen through clenched teeth. Immediately she ordered one of the older ladies-in-waiting to sit by her bed all night, to find out whether the dream was simply a dream or whether it was real.

The soldier wanted so much to see the beautiful Princess again that he sent tea-cup eyes to fetch her to him. Sure enough, the dog picked her up and and ran back for all he was worth. The old lady was equal to the task. She put on her boots and chased the dog all the way to the soldier's lodgings. When she saw the dog disappear inside, the old lady took out a piece of chalk and drew a large cross on the door so that she would be able to find the place next morning. She returned to the Copper Castle and, later on, the dog brought the Princess back too.

As you know, this was no ordinary dog: he noticed the chalk mark on the door of the soldier's lodgings. So he took a piece of chalk and put a cross on the door of every house in the town – the old lady would never remember which door it was now.

Next morning the King, the Queen, the old lady-in-waiting and the Royal Guard set out to look for the house where the Princess had been.

'This is it!' exclaimed the King, pointing at a large cross on a door.

'I don't think so, husband dear,' said the Queen, indicating another cross.

'But here's another, and another and another,' everyone chorused. And so they realised that their search was pointless.

Now the Queen was really a very clever person. She took her big golden scissors and cut out some pieces of silk and sewed them together to make a beautiful little bag. She filled the bag with small grains of wheat and tied it round the Princess's waist as she slept. Then she cut a tiny hole in the bag so that the grains would drop out and leave a trail showing where the Princess went.

Later that night the dog arrived and carried the Princess on his back to the soldier, who by now was so head over heels in love with her that he wanted to marry her and be her Prince Charming.

The dog did not notice the fine grains of wheat which left a trail from the castle to the soldier's window. And so it was that early next morning the King and Queen discovered where their daughter had been. They arrested the soldier and threw him in prison.

There he sat. How dark and depressing the whole thing was. But worse was to follow: a message came through, 'You will hang tomorrow morning.' That was all he needed. Worse still, he had left his tinderbox back at his lodgings.

As he looked out between the bars of his cell-window the next morning, he saw crowds of people rushing off to see his execution. He heard drums and saw soldiers marching. Everybody was going. Then he spied a young shoemaker's apprentice still wearing his apron and slippers. The lad was running for all he was worth when one of his slippers suddenly flew off. It came to rest just by the soldier's window.

'Hey, laddie, what's all the rush? Nothing will happen until I get there. Listen, how about doing me a favour? Nip into my lodgings and fetch me my tinderbox, will you. I'll make it worth your while – four shillings – but, please, get a move on.'

The young apprentice grabbed the money, quickly went and found the tinderbox, gave it to the soldier and...and so to the climax of our tale.

On the outskirts of town stood a huge gallows guarded by soldiers. There was already a huge crowd of spectators: hundreds of thousands of them. The King and Queen were there too and sat on a beautiful throne just above the judge and the rest of the court officials.

The soldier was brought onto the gallows and the noose was made ready for his neck. Suddenly the soldier spoke up. Was it not customary for the condemned man to have one last request before he met his maker? After all, he only wanted a last pipe of tobacco.

The King could not turn him down. So the soldier took out his tinderbox and struck it once, twice, three times! And there stood the dogs: teacup, millstone and old Round Tower himself, all three!

'Help me – they're going to hang me!' shouted the soldier and immediately the dogs rushed at the judge and the court officials and tossed them high into the sky. They came down with a deathly crash.

'No – not me,' screamed the King, but the largest of the dogs picked up both the King and Queen and threw them even higher in the air. When the soldiers saw this, they threw down their weapons and ran for it. The people shouted, 'Dear, sweet soldier, be our King and you may take the beautiful Princess for your bride.'

So the soldier got into the King's carriage and the three dogs marched in front shouting, 'Hurrah!' The crowd waved and cheered and the soldier waved back. The Princess came out of the Copper Castle and became his Queen (she didn't mind this in the slightest). The wedding celebrations lasted for eight days and the three dogs sat up at the table too, and made eyes at everyone.

The Magic Ring

ONE NIGHT AS the King of the Mountains lay sleeping he dreamed that a spirit appeared to him in the darkness.

'O King,' the spirit told him, 'tomorrow morning when the sun is still low, mount your horse and ride southwards, through the narrow pass that divides the mountains. You will come to a place where the mountains are steep, and there are caves. Then your horse will stop, refusing to go on. Wherever the horse stops, you must dig until you come to an underground passage.'

'And then?' the King heard himself asking, still asleep.

'You will come to an open space under the ground, where much treasure is to be found. In the centre of that cavern stands a brass statue, and on the statue's finger is a ring. When you touch it, the statue will cry out. Pay

11

no attention, and do not fear. Take the ring from the statue and slip it on your own finger.'

'What is the special virtue of this ring?'

'As long as you wear it, you are safe from any harm. Whenever you take it off a Jinn will appear, ready to obey your orders. And if you place it in your mouth you will immediately become invisible.'

When he woke up the King was troubled by this dream, which was very vivid. For dreams may come either from Allah or from Satan, and he was afraid that if he did as the spirit ordered him he might find himself in the hands of the devil, bound by evil magic. When morning came, he did nothing about it. In fact, he took care not even to mount his horse that day, lest the animal carry him away into the mountains.

On the following night the same thing happened, and the same spirit spoke the same words. And so it was on the third night. Then the King concluded that these words were indeed the words of Allah. Next morning he rose with the sun, mounted his horse, and turned to face to the south.

He rode alone through the narrow pass, where the mountains were steep, and he could see caves on either side. Then his horse stopped, suddenly, and would go no farther.

'This must be the place,' the King thought to himself. He took the spade he had brought with him, and dug exactly where the horse had stopped, and it was not long before he uncovered a trap-door. He opened the door and saw that a flight of steps led down into the darkness below, whereupon he took his candle and followed the steps until they brought him out into a long underground passage. This in turn led him into a great cavern, which must have been far inside the mountains.

He could see the sparkle of gold in the shadows around him, but he paid no attention to the treasure. In the centre of the cavern stood a great brass statue, life size, with one hand holding a brass sword and the other hand outstretched towards the entrance of the cave; on the finger of that hand he could see a golden ring. Taking courage from his dream, the King began to pull the ring off the brass finger.

At once there was a great outcry. The figure screamed as though it were human, and its metallic cries echoed and rebounded off the walls of the cavern until it seemed as though an army of men were shouting. Terrified, the King nevertheless managed to seize the ring, and no sooner was it on his own finger than the noise ceased and the statue simply fell apart in front of his eyes, leaving nothing but a scattered heap of brass.

The King fled from the haunted cave as quickly as he could, but as soon as he was safely back in daylight he took the ring off his finger and held it in his hand. Immediately a tall, dark figure appeared in front of him.

'I am Maimoun, the Jinn,' he said. 'Command me.'

'Carry the treasure from the underground cavern into the treasury of my palace,' ordered the King.

'It is done,' said Maimoun, and disappeared.

Then the King placed the ring in his mouth. At once he was invisible; he held out his hand and could not see it, and he looked down at his feet and they were not there. Well content, he replaced the ring on his finger, mounted his horse, and rode home.

The King kept this magic ring secret, even from his three sons, and only occasionally made use of its powers. But many years later, when he knew that he had not much longer to live, he called his sons to him one by one.

'You will inherit my throne, and half of my fortune,' he said to the eldest, who was well pleased.

'And you will inherit the other half of my fortune,' he said to the second, who was well pleased.

Then the third son Ali, who had already heard of these promises, came in to his father. 'Father, what have you done?' he asked reproachfully. 'Have you forgotten that you have three sons, that you now divide your kingdom in half?'

'I have not forgotten, my son. Your portion is worth more than the whole of my kingdom, for although I love your brothers well I love you best of all. Yet this you must keep for ever secret, or I fear for your life.' Then he gave Ali the ring, explaining its magic powers.

So the King died. His eldest son inherited the throne, and for some years all went well. The brothers lived at peace together, not envying each other's inheritance. Ali secretly tried out his ring, to make sure that it was as wonderful as his father had said, but after that he seldom used it; he had simple tastes and no wish to acquire great wealth.

Then one day Ali saw that the new King, his elder brother, was gravely worried. He would scarcely eat or drink, his forehead was clouded and he sighed constantly.

'What ails you, my brother,' he chided him. 'Is it so difficult to be a king?'

'Indeed it is,' the King replied, not smiling. 'For I fear that our kingdom is in great danger.'

'Danger from what?' asked Ali.

'Danger from outside,' the King told him. 'As you know, there is a Christian King whose lands lie between us and the sea, and now this King has raised an army several thousand strong and is attacking our northern frontier. He seems to be driven simply by love of power and of conquest, and will let nothing stand in his way.'

Ali laughed. 'Give me ten minutes and I will bring you this Christian King, in chains.'

He went aside into his own room and took off his ring. When Maimoun the Jinn appeared he ordered him to transport the Christian King to the palace, chained, and immediately it was done. Then Ali took the unfortunate monarch into the throne room, and commanded him to fall at his brother's feet.

When the latter had recovered from his surprise and realised that by some miracle his enemy was at his mercy, he reproached the prisoner. 'My people have never done you harm,' he said, 'and you have a great kingdom of your own. Why then have you attacked mine?'

'How could I know that you were protected by magic, and that a Jinn was your servant?' cried the Christian, although this did not exactly answer the question.

Then he begged the King's pardon, swearing on oath that if he were set free he would be the King's vassal for life.

'You are free,' said the King magnanimously, and motioned to his slaves to remove the chains from the prisoner. But they could not. One after another tried to unlock them, or cut through the metal, but in vain.

'I think that only he who chained me can free me,' the Christian King told them. Then Ali reached out and touched the chains, and they vanished.

'Now you are free to return whence you came,' the King told him.

'How on earth am I to get there?' the Christian protested. 'Do you not know that my country is three months' journey from here, by the fastest horse? Long before I could reach home my people would think me dead, and there would be a new ruler.'

The King turned to Ali. 'You brought him here,' he said; 'send him home.'

Ali took the unfortunate ruler away into his own room, removed his ring, and ordered Maimoun to carry the Christian back again to his own capital. But by this time of course Ali's two older brothers knew that their youngest brother had some magic far greater than anything they had dreamed of. They were afraid, for they also knew now that if he wanted the throne, or their fortunes, or anything else in the wold, he could take it.

'We must discover the secret of this magic,' the King told his other brother.

'Leave it to me,' said the second brother. 'But first of all let us order a great feast to be held tonight, for all our people, to celebrate our deliverance from the Christian army.'

So that night a banquet was prepared in the palace. The dishes were set out in long rows, with room for five hundred men to sit. There were whole roast sheep lying on huge platters of rice, coloured yellow with saffron; there were vine-leaves and peppers and egg-plants stuffed with different kinds of meat, there were chickens, and bowls of tasty sauces into which people dipped their bread. Only one thing was lacking.

'Alas,' said the second brother to his youngest brother Ali, 'if only we had lemons such as grow in Baghdad, it would give taste to the meat.'

'I can get you lemons from Baghdad,' said Ali, and without stopping to think he took the ring from his finger. At once Maimoun stood beside him. 'Bring us a dozen of the best lemons that grow in Baghdad,' he commanded, and within a minute the lemons were on the table.

The King and his second brother exchanged glances. Later that night, when all the guests had gone, they met and whispered together, plotting to get rid of Ali and obtain the magic ring for themselves. But one of the serving women in the palace, who had been Ali's nurse, overheard them and hurried to tell the young Prince that he was in danger.

'If that is so,' said Ali, 'I will leave my brothers, and my home, and set off to see the world.' He took the ring from his finger, and Maimoun immediately stood beside him.

'Tell me, Maimoun,' he said. 'What is the most beautiful country in the world?'

'The Isle of Camphor, that lies in the Red Sea.'

'And who is the most beautiful girl in the world?'

'Princess Fatima, the daughter of the King of the Isle of Camphor. Her skin is white, her lips are red, her hair is black.'

'Take me to the Island,' said Ali.

The Jinn swept him away across the mountains, across the eastern desert, and along the sea coast, and so they landed on the Isle of Camphor. It was like a garden, with trees and flowers and a scent of spices in the air, and the blue sea touching it on every side. There was a town, its white houses shining in the sun, and outside the town was a large, walled palace.

Ali slipped his ring into his mouth, so that he was invisible, and then he made his way inside the palace walls. He wandered through courtyards and gardens until at last he found the Princess Fatima sitting beside a pool with one of her handmaidens, whose name was Selwa. He looked at her and saw that she was indeed more beautiful than any maiden he had ever seen before.

Next day Ali, dressed like a prince, and riding a handsome black horse, presented himself at the palace and introduced himself to the King as a Prince from a far distant country. 'I have come to ask for the hand of your daughter in marriage,' he said.

The King laughed. 'So have many other princes, rich merchants, and kings,' he said. 'But the Princess Fatima is hard to please. She swears that she will only marry a man who will bring her lemons from Baghdad, mangoes from the Nile, and dates from Medina, all in the same season.'

'So be it,' Ali agreed. 'Tomorrow she shall have the lemons, the mangoes and the dates.'

On the following morning Ali presented himself again at the palace. He was followed by three slaves, each one carrying a huge silver platter on his head, one with lemons from Baghdad, one with mangoes from the Nile, one with dates from Medina. The King was delighted and ordered that the wedding should take place that very night, followed by three days of feasting for all the people of the Island, and he proclaimed Ali his son and heir. But the Princess Fatima was so angry that her dark eyes grew darker and her red lips grew pale, for she had not intended to marry any man; she had only set her three conditions to make it impossible, and now she could not break her promise, even though she knew that the conditions must have been fulfilled by magic.

Ali and the Princess were married that night. But Fatima, who hated her husband, as she hated all men, vowed to herself there and then that she would discover the secret of his magic and steal it from him. She watched him every day, every hour, every minute, and she never ceased asking him to do impossible things for her, to bring her delicacies from all over the world, to bring her horses from Arabia and silks from Damascus and pearls from India. Ali was very careful, and he would always shut himself in his own room before he took off the magic ring and summoned Maimoun to do his bidding. But then one day he did not fasten his door securely. Fatima opened it a crack, very quietly, and watched him hold the magic ring, and saw what happened.

She could scarcely wait until Ali was asleep that night before she slipped the ring from his finger and on to her own. Then she took it off and held it in her hand, and the Jinn immediately appeared before her. 'Take this man and carry him back to wherever he came from,' she ordered, pointing at Ali, and Maimoun heard the hatred in her voice. He hesitated, for he had grown as fond of Ali as a Jinn could do of his master, but he was bound by the power of the ring. He swept Ali away across the sea, across the eastern mountains and the desert to his own country and left him there.

So Ali woke up in the palace of his two brothers, without the ring. They welcomed him with open arms, for they had long since repented of their plan to kill him, and they urged him to stay with them and to forget the Isle of Camphor and the magic ring. They had land and treasure enough for all three, they said. But he would not listen.

'I must have my ring,' he told them, 'for it is my heritage. I dare not leave it in the hands of the Princess Fatima, who is as evil as she is beautiful.'

He took his horse and a bag of gold, and rode three months before he reached the seashore. There he took ship and travelled another three months before he reached Suez and the Red Sea. At Suez he heard news from the Isle of Camphor, where it seemed that the Princess Fatima had murdered her father and seized the throne. Moreover, she would allow no man to enter the kingdom, only women, and any ship that called there was searched for strangers.

When he heard this Ali knew that the Princess was afraid he would return, and he took heart. He found the captain of a small ship that traded in spices with the Isle of Camphor, gave him all that was left of his gold, and persuaded him to let him travel on the ship, disguised as a slave woman, veiled from head to foot. So he came ashore on the Island, unnoticed, with other women, and found lodgings in the town.

Ali soon discovered that the people hated their new ruler. The Princess was cruel and extravagant. She had killed most of her father's old and faithful advisers, and no one dared speak to her or tell her when things were going badly on the Island. People no longer smiled, and they spoke in whispers, afraid of being overheard.

One day as he stood near the palace gate Ali saw Selwa, who was the handmaiden of the Princess, come out. Taking his courage in his hands, he followed her, and as soon as they were out of sight of the palace he threw back his woman's veil and greeted her.

'Peace be with you,' he said. 'I am Ali, who was the husband of your Princess.'

'Thanks be to Allah!' she cried, delighted . 'It is well that you have come back, for there is much unhappiness in the palace.'

'Will you help me?' Ali asked her.

'I will help you.'

'Then you must do exactly as I tell you. Next time you are in the Princess's room you must pretend to be taken ill, so ill that you cannot be moved and can only lie on the couch in her own room. When the Princess and the doctors ask what ails you, you must say that only fresh lemons from Baghdad will cure you. Then watch what happens, and come back and tell me.'

Selwa went back into the palace, and found the Princess in her room. She sat down at her feet, pretending to be busy with some embroidery, and then suddenly she put her hand to her heart and cried out that she was ill. Alarmed, the Princess made her lie down on her own couch and quickly summoned a doctor, who felt her hands and her head and the beat of her heart.

'I find nothing wrong,' he said, and then to Selwa – 'What is it that ails you?'

'I am faint and cannot lift my head,' she said, 'and I know of only one thing that will cure me.'

'What is that?'

'Fresh lemons from Baghdad.'

When she heard this, the Princess dismissed the doctor. 'Close your eyes, she said to the girl, ' and do not open them until I tell you, for if you do even fresh lemons will not cure you.'

Then the Princess took out a narrow ladder from her cupboard, placed it against the wall, and climbed up until she could reach a shelf above the door of the room. She took down a golden casket, opened it, and took out an ivory box. She opened the ivory box, and took out a ring. She held the ring in her hands, and the Jinn appeared, and no sooner had she told him what she wanted than she had a whole bowl of lemons from Baghdad.

Although her eyes were apparently closed, Selwa had been able to see all this through her long eyeslashes. Now she closed her eyes tighter and when the Princess spoke to her she opened them very suddenly, exclaiming with astonishment and delight at the sight of the lemons.

Next day she met Ali again outside the palace, and told him exactly what had happened. 'Bring me the ring,' he said.

Selwa waited until a day when she was sure that the Princess would be away from the palace for some time. Then she took the ladder, climbed up, and opened the gold casket, opened the ivory box, and took out the ring. She slipped it quickly on her own finger, for she was fearful of magic and had no wish to summon up a Jinn, and took it to Ali.

'Now,' he said, 'go back into the palace and pretend that nothing has happened. I will follow you.'

As soon as he was alone Ali summoned Maimoun and, with his aid, dressed himself again as a prince. The he placed the ring in his mouth, becoming invisible, and made his way past all the sentries and guards into the palace, where he slipped the ring again on his finger. He found the Princess in her room.

'In the name of Allah, greetings,' he said.

'How dare you come here?' she said, startled. 'Go back to your own country at once and leave me in peace.'

'This is my country,' he told her. 'Your father the King accepted me as his heir, and now that he is dead, murdered by you, I have come to take the throne.'

The Princess said nothing. Instead she ran to the cupboard and took out the ladder, placed it against the wall, and climbed up to get the golden casket. She opened it, opened the ivory box, and found nothing.

'I have the ring on my finger,' Ali told her.

Then the Princess screamed and rushed for the door, calling for her guards, but Ali stood in the way. 'What is the use of guards?' he asked her. 'You know that for every man in your army, I can call a thousand.'

He turned the ring in his hand, and Maimoun stood beside him. 'What should we do with a Princess who is so beautiful and so evil?'

'Master, I cannot say. I can only obey.'

'I will not kill her, for she was my wife,' said Ali. 'But I cannot leave her free, who knows the secret of the ring.'

Maimoun stood silent.

'Carry her away then, to the cave where my father found the statue wearing this ring,' Ali commanded him. 'Put her to sleep there, so that she will sleep for a thousand years.'

The Jinn and the Princess vanished almost as he finished speaking, and Ali put the ring back on his finger. Thereafter he reigned in peace as the King of the Isle of Camphor, and the people rejoiced. He married the hand-maiden Selwa, who was almost as beautiful as the Princess, and very much nicer, and they lived happily the rest of their lives.

As for the wicked Princess Fatima, she still lies sleeping in the cave in the mountains. Only Allah knows what will happen when at last she wakes up. But she has three hundred and ninety-nine years yet to sleep.

The Creation of Man

*O*ne *dark and starry night a group of American Indians sat huddled round a fire. Suddenly the oldest warrior stood up. His face was as old and as brown as the earth, and round his shoulders he wore a brightly-coloured blanket. He began to tell the story about the beginning of the world...*

"When Coyote, the desert dog, finished making the world, he took the wind, which was shaped like a sea-shell, and turned it upside down to form the sky. He put bright colours at the five corners of the world and a rainbow sprang up overhead and divided the night from the day. Then he sat back on his haunches and howled – and the sun and moon began to move across the sky.

Coyote planted the plains with trees and ponds and mountains and rivers, and he made all the animals.

25

'Last and best of all, I shall make *Man*,' Coyote thought aloud. But the animals heard him and wanted to help. So they all sat down in a circle in the forest: Coyote, Grizzly Bear, Lion, Honey Bear, Deer, Sheep, Beaver, Owl and Mouse.

'You can make Man whatever shape you like,' said Lion, 'but I think he should have sharp teeth for tearing meat, and long claws, too.'

'Like yours?' asked Coyote.

'Well, yes. Like mine,' said Lion. 'He will need fur, of course. And a big, loud, roaring voice.'

'Like yours?' asked Coyote.

'Like mine,' said Lion.

'Nobody wants a voice like yours,' Grizzly interrupted. 'You frighten everyone away. Man must be able to walk on his back legs and creep up on things and hug them in his arms until they're squashed flat.'

'Like you do?' asked Coyote.

'Well, yes. Like I do,' replied Grizzly.

Deer, who trembled nervously and kept glancing over her shoulder, said: 'What's all this about tearing meat and squashing things? It isn't nice. Man has to be able to know when he's in danger and run away quickly. He should have ears like sea-shells to hear every tiny sound. And eyes like the Moon, which sees everything. Oh, and antlers, of course. He will need antlers.'

'Like yours?' asked Coyote.

'Well, yes. Like mine,' said Deer.

'Like *yours*?' scoffed Sheep. 'What good are antlers? Long, spiky things that get caught in every branch and bush! How is Man going to be able to *butt* things? Now if he had horns on either side of his head…'

'Like yours?' asked Coyote.

Sheep only sniffed. He did not like being interrupted.

Then Beaver stood up and said: 'You are forgetting the most important thing of all – Man's *tail*. Long thin tails are all right for swatting flies, I suppose. But Man must have a broad, flat tail. How else can he build dams in the river?'

'Like yours?' asked Coyote.

'Nobody builds dams like *mine*,' said the Beaver, in a very boastful way.

'Man sounds far too *big*,' squeaked Mouse. 'He would be better being small.'

'You're all out of your wits-wits-woo!" hooted Owl. 'What about wings? If you want Man to be the best animal of all, he must be able to fly. He *must have wings*!'

'Like yours?' asked Coyote.

'Is that all you can say?' Owl complained. 'Don't you have any ideas?'

Coyote jumped to his feet and prowled to the centre of the circle. 'You silly animals! I don't know what I was thinking about when I made you! You all want Man to look exactly like you!'

'And I suppose Man should be just like *you*, Coyote,' growled Honey Bear.

'Then how could anyone tell us apart?' replied Coyote. 'Everyone would point at me and say, "There goes Man". And they would point at Man and say, "There goes Coyote". No, no. Man must be *different*.'

'But with a tail!' shouted Beaver. 'And wings!' hooted Owl. 'And antlers!' bayed Deer. 'And horns!' baaed Sheep. 'And a roar!' roared Grizzly. 'And be very small,' squeaked Mouse. But nobody heard him. They were too busy fighting.

Biting and butting and clawing and chewing, the animals fought each other across the forest floor while Coyote stood by and shook his head. Fur and feathers and hooves and horns flew all over the place.

Coyote picked them up, and putting them together again he made all sorts of new, peculiar animals – like the camel and the giraffe.

Soon all the animals lay in an exhausted heap, too tired to fight any more. 'I think I may have the answer,' said Coyote at last.

The animals blinked at him, and some of them snarled. But Coyote spoke to them all the same.

'Bear was right to say that Man should walk on his back legs. That means he can reach into the trees. And Deer was right to say that Man should have sharp ears and good eyes. But if Man had wings he would bump his head on the sky. The only part of a bird that he needs is Eagle's long claws. I think I'll call them fingers.

'And Lion was right when he said that Man should have a big voice. But he needs a little voice, too, so that he's not too frightening. I think Man should be smooth like Fish, who has no fur to make him hot and itchy. But most important of all,' said Coyote finally, 'Man must be more clever and cunning than *any* of you!'

'Like you are,' muttered all the animals.

'Well, yes, thank you.' said Coyote. 'Like I am.' There was a lot of angry growling and hissing and the animals began to shout: 'Sit down Coyote! Nobody likes your silly ideas!'

'Well,' said Coyote patiently. 'Let's have a competition. We'll each make a model of Man out of mud. Tomorrow we can look at all the models and decide which is the best.'

So all the animals rushed away to fetch water and make mud. Owl made a model with wings. Deer made a model with large ears and wide eyes. Beaver made a model with a broad, flat tail. Mouse made a very small model. But Coyote made Man.

The sun went down before any of them could finish their models. So they went to sleep on the forest floor. All except Coyote.

He fetched water from the river and poured it over all the other models. Beaver's mud tail was washed away. Deer's mud antlers were washed away. Owl's mud wings were washed away.

Coyote blew into the nose of his model of Man made of mud. And when the other animals woke up, they found that there was a new animal in the forest. His name was Man."

With these words the old warrior sat down, wrapping his blanket round him. As the glow from the fire died down, he sat as silent as the earth staring into the darkness. And in the distance the cry of the coyote floated across the plains.

From Tiger to Anansi

ONCE UPON A time and a long long time ago the Tiger was king of the forest.

At evening when all the animals sat together in a circle and talked and laughed together, Snake would ask:

'Who is the strongest of us all?'

'Tiger is strongest,' cried Dog. 'When Tiger whispers the trees listen. When Tiger is angry and cries out, the trees tremble.'

'And who is the weakest of all?' asked Snake.

'Anansi,' shouted Dog, and they all laughed together. 'Anansi the spider is weakest of all. When he whispers no one listens. When he shouts everyone laughs.'

Now one day the weakest and strongest came face to face, Anansi and Tiger. They met in a clearing of the forest. The frogs hiding under the cool leaves saw them. The bright-green parrots in the branches heard them.

When they met, Anansi bowed so low that his forehead touched the ground. Tiger did not greet him. Tiger just looked at Anansi.

'Good morning, Tiger,' cried Anansi. 'I have a favour to ask.'

'And what is it, Anansi?' said Tiger.

'Tiger, we all know that you are strongest of us all. This is why we give your name to many things. We have Tiger lilies and Tiger stories and Tiger moths, and Tiger this and Tiger that. Everyone knows that I am weakest of all. This is why nothing bears my name. Tiger, let something be called after the weakest one so that men may know my name too.'

'Well,' said Tiger, without so much as a glance toward Anansi, 'what would you like to bear your name?'

'The stories,' cried Anansi. 'The stories that we tell in the forest evening at time when the sun goes down, the stories about Br'er Snake and Br'er Tacumah, Br'er Cow and Br'er Bird and all of us.'

Now Tiger liked these stories and he meant to keep them as Tiger stories. He thought to himself, how stupid, how weak this Anansi is. I will play a trick on him so that all the animals will laugh at him. Tiger moved his tail slowly from side to side and said, 'Very good, Anansi, very good. I will let the stories be named after you, if you do what I ask.'

'Tiger, I will do what you ask.'

'Yes, I am sure you will, I am sure you will,' said Tiger, moving his tail slowly from side to side. 'It is a little thing that I ask. Bring me Mr Snake alive. Do you know Snake who lives down by the river, Mr Anansi? Bring him to me alive and you can have the stories.'

Tiger stopped speaking. He did not move his tail. He looked at Anansi and waited for him to speak. All the animals in the forest waited. Mr Frog beneath the cool leaves, Mr Parrot up in the tree, all watched Anansi. They were all ready to laugh at him.

'Tiger, I will do what you ask,' said Anansi. At these words a great wave of laughter burst from the forest. The frogs and parrots laughed. Tiger laughed loudest of all, for how could feeble Anansi catch Snake alive?

Anansi went away. He heard the forest laughing at him from every side.

That was on Monday morning. Anansi sat before his house and thought of plan after plan. At last he hit upon one that could not fail. He would build a Calaban.

On Tuesday morning Anansi built a Calaban. He took a strong vine and made a noose. He hid the vine in the grass. Inside the noose he set some of the berries that Snake loved best. Then he waited. Soon Snake came up the path. He saw the berries and went toward them. He lay across the vine and ate the berries. Anansi pulled at the vine to tighten the noose, but Snake's body was too heavy. Anansi saw that the Calaban had failed.

Wednesday came. Anansi made a deep hole in the ground. He made the sides slippery with grease. In the bottom he put some of the bananas that Snake loved. Then he hid in the bush beside the road and waited.

Snake came crawling down the path toward the river. He was hungry and thirsty. He saw the bananas at the bottom of the hole. He saw that the sides of the hole were slippery. First he wrapped his tail tightly round the trunk of a tree, then he reached down into the hole and ate the bananas. When he was finished he pulled himself up by his tail and crawled away. Anansi had lost his bananas and he had lost Snake, too.

Thursday morning came. Anansi made a Fly Up. Inside the trap he put an egg. Snake came down the path. He was happy this morning, so happy that he lifted his head and a third of his long body from the ground. He just lowered his head, took up the egg in his mouth, and never ever touched the trap. The Fly Up could not catch Snake.

What was Anansi to do? Friday morning came. He sat and thought all day. It was no use.

Now it was Saturday morning. This was the last day. Anansi went for a walk down by the river. He passed by the hole where Snake lived. There was Snake, his body hidden in the hole, his head resting on the ground at the entrance to the hole. It was early morning. Snake was watching the sun rise above the mountains.

'Good morning, Anansi,' said Snake.

'Good morning, Snake,' said Anansi.

'Anansi, I am very angry with you. You have been trying to catch me all week. You set a Fly Up to catch me. The day before you made a Slippery Hole for me. The day before that you made a Calaban. I have a good mind to kill you, Anansi.'

'Ah, you are too clever, Snake,' said Anansi. 'You are much too clever. Yes, what you say is so. I tried to catch you, but I failed. Now I can never prove that you are the longest animal in the world, longer even than the bamboo tree.'

'Of course I am the longest of all animals,' cried Snake. 'I am much longer than the bamboo tree.'

'What, longer than that bamboo trees across there? asked Anansi.

'Of course I am,' said Snake. 'Look and see.' Snake came out of the hole and stretched himself out at full length.

'Yes, you are very, very long,' said Anansi 'but the bamboo tree is very long, too. Now that I look at you and at the bamboo tree I must say that the bamboo tree seems longer. But it's hard to say because it is further away.'

'Well, bring it nearer,' cried Snake. 'Cut it down and put it beside me. You will soon see that I am much longer.'

Anansi ran to the bamboo tree and cut it down. He placed it on the ground and cut off all its branches. Bush, bush, bush, bush! There it was, long and straight as a flagstaff.

'Now put it beside me,' said Snake.

Anansi put the long bamboo tree down on the ground beside Snake. Then he said:

'Snake, when I go up to see where your head is, you will crawl up. When I go down to see where your tail is, you will crawl down. In that way you will always seem to be longer than the bamboo tree, which really is longer than you are.'

'Tie my tail, then!' said Snake. 'Tie my tail! I know that I am longer than the bamboo, whatever you say.'

Anansi tied Snake's tail to the end of the bamboo. Then he ran up to the other end.

'Stretch, Snake, stretch, and we will see who is longer.'

A crowd of animals were gathering round. Here was something better than a race. 'Stretch, Snake, stretch,' they called.

Snake stretched as hard as he could. Anansi tied him round his middle so that he should not slip back. Now one more try. Snake knew that if he stretched hard enough he would prove to be longer than the bamboo.

Anansi ran up to him. 'Rest yourself for a little, Snake, and then stretch again. If you can stretch another six inches you will be longer than the bamboo. Try your hardest. Stretch so that you even have to shut your eyes. Ready?'

'Yes,' said Snake. Then Snake made a mighty effort. He stretched so hard that he had to squeeze his eyes shut. 'Hooray!' cried the animals. 'You are winning, Snake. Just two inches more.'

And at that moment Anansi tied Snake's head to the bamboo. There he was. At last he had caught Snake, all by himself.

The animals fell silent. Yes, there Snake was, all tied up, ready to be taken to Tiger. And feeble Anansi had done this. They could laugh at him no more.

And never again did Tiger dare to call these stories by his name. They were Anansi stories for ever after, from that day to this.

David and Goliath
(from the Good News Bible)

Goliath Challenges the Israelites

THE PHILISTINES GATHERED for battle in Socoh, a town in Judah; they camped at a place called Ephes Dammim, between Socoh and Azekah. ²Saul and the Israelites assembled and camped in the Valleh of Elah, where they got ready to fight the Philistines. ³The Philistines lined up on one hill and the Israelites on another, with a valley between them.

4 A man named Goliath, from the city of Gath, came out from the Philistine camp to challenge the Israelites. He was nearly three metres tall ⁵and wore bronze armour that weighed about fifty-seven kilogrammes and a bronze helmet. ⁶His legs were also protected by bronze armour, and he carried a bronze javelin slung over his shoulder. ⁷His spear was as thick as the bar on a weaver's loom, and its iron head weighed about seven kilo-

grammes. A soldier walked in front of him carrying his shield. ⁸Goliath stood and shouted at the Israelites, 'What are you doing there, lined up for battle? I am a Philistine, you slaves of Saul! Choose one of your men to fight me. ⁹If he wins and kills me, we will be your slaves; but if I win and kill him, you will be our slaves. ¹⁰Here and now I challenge the Israelite army. I dare you to pick someone to fight me!' ¹¹When Saul and his men heard this, they were terrified.

David in Saul's Camp

12 David was the son of Jesse, who was an Ephrathite from Bethlehem in Judah. Jesse had eight sons, and at the time Saul was king, he was already a very old man. ¹³His three eldest sons had gone with Saul to war. The eldest was Eliab, the next was Abinadab, and the third was Shammah. ¹⁴David was the youngest son, and while the three eldest brothers stayed with Saul, ¹⁵David would go back to Bethlehem from time to time, to take care of his father's sheep.

16 Goliath challenged the Israelites every morning and evening for forty days.

17 One day Jesse said to David, 'Take ten kilogrammes of this roasted grain and these ten loaves of bread, and hurry with them to your brothers in the camp. ¹⁸And take these ten cheeses to the commanding officer. Find out how your brothers are getting on and bring back something to show that you saw them and that they are well. ¹⁹King Saul, your brotners, and all the other Israelites are in the Valley of Elah fighting the Philistines.'

20 David got up early the next morning, left someone

else in charge of the sheep, took the food, and went as Jesse had told him to. He arrived at the camp just as the Israelites were going out to their battle line, shouting the war-cry. [21]The Philistine and the Israelite armies took up positions for battle, facing each other. [22]David left the food with the officer in charge of the supplies, ran to the battle line, went to his brothers, and asked how they were getting on. [23]As he was talking to them, Goliath came forward and challenged the Israelites as he had done before. And David heard him. [24]When the Israelites saw Goliath, they ran away in terror .[25]'Look at him!' they said to each other. 'Listen to his challenge! King Saul has promised to give a big reward to the man who kills him; the king will also give him his daughter to marry and will not require his father's family to pay taxes.'

26 David asked the men who were near him, 'What will the man get who kills this Philistine and frees Israel from this disgrace? After all, who is this heathen Philistine to defy the army of the living God?' [27]They told him what would be done for the man who killed Goliath.

28 Eliab, David's eldest brother, heard David talking to the men. He was angry with David and said, 'What are you doing here? Who is taking care of those sheep of yours out there in the wilderness? You cheeky brat, you! You just came to watch the fighting!'

29 'Now what have I done?' David asked. 'Can't I even ask a question?'

30 He turned to another man and asked him the same question, and every time he asked, he got the same answer.

31 Some men heard what David had said, and they told Saul, who sent for him. [32]David said to Saul, 'Your Majesty, no one should be afraid of this Philistine! I will go and fight him.'

33 'No,' answered Saul. 'How could you fight him? You're just a boy, and he has been a soldier all his life!'

34 'You Majesty,' David said, 'I take care of my father's sheep. Whenever a lion or a bear carries off a lamb, [35]I go after it, attack it, and rescue the lamb. And if the lion or bear turns on me, I grab it by the throat and beat it to death. [36]I have killed lions and bears, and I will do the same to this heathen Philistine, who has defied the army of the living God. [37]The LORD has saved me from lions and bears; he will save me from this Philistine.'

'All right,' Saul answered. 'Go, and the LORD be with you.' [38]He gave his own armour to David for him to wear: a bronze helmet, which he put on David's head, and a coat of armour. [39]David strapped Saul's sword over the armour and tried to walk, but he couldn't, because he wasn't used to wearing them. 'I can't fight with all this,' he said to Saul. 'I'm not used to it.' So he took it all off. [40]He took his shepherd's stick and then picked up five smooth stones from the stream and put them in his bag. With his catapult ready, he went out to meet Goliath.

David Defeats Goliath

41 The Philistine started walking towards David, with his shield-bearer walking in front of him. He kept coming closer, [42]and when he got a good look at David, he was filled with scorn for him because he was just a

nice, good-looking boy. [43]He said to David, 'What's that stick for? Do you think I'm a dog?' And he called down curses from his god on David. [44]'Come on,' he challenged David, 'and I will give your body to the birds and animals to eat.'

45 David answered, 'You are coming against me with sword, spear, and javelin, but I come against you in the name of the LORD Almighty, the God of the Israelite armies, which you have defied. [46]This very day the LORD will put you in my power; I will defeat you and cut off your head. And I will give the bodies of the Philistine soldiers to the birds and animals to eat. Then the whole world will know that Israel has a God, [47]and everyone here will see that the LORD does not need swords or spears to save his people. He is victorious in battle, and he will put all of you in our power.'

48 Goliath started walking towards David again, and David ran quickly towards the Philistine battle line to fight him. [49]He put his hand into his bag and took out a stone, which he slung at Goliath. It hit him on the forehead and broke his skull, and Goliath fell face downwards on the ground. [50]And so, without a sword, David defeated and killed Goliath with a catapult and a stone! [51]He ran to him, stood over him, took Goliath's sword out of its sheath, and cut off his head and killed him.

When the Philistines saw that their hero was dead, they ran away. [52]The men of Israel and Judah shouted and ran after them, pursuing them all the way to Gath and to the gates of Ekron. The Philistines fell wounded all along the road that leads to Shaaraim, as far as Gath and Ekron. [53]When the Israelites came back from pursuing the Philistines, they looted their camp. [54]David picked up Goliath's head and took it to Jerusalem, but he kept Goliath's weapons in his own tent.

David Is Presented to Saul

55 When Saul saw David going out to fight Goliath, he asked Abner, the commander of his army, 'Abner, whose son is he?'

'I have no idea, Your Majesty,' Abner answered.

56 'Then go and find out,' Saul ordered.

57 So when David returned to camp after killing Goliath, Abner took him to Saul. David was still carrying Goliath's head. [58]Saul asked him, 'Young man, whose son are you?'

'I am the son of your servant Jesse from Bethlehem,' David answered.

David and Goliath
(from the James I Bible)

NOW THE PHILISTINES gathered together their armies to battle, and were gathered together at Shochoh, which *belongeth* to Judah, and pitched between Shochoh and Azekah, in Ephes-dammim.

2 And Saul and the men of Israel were gathered together, and pitched by the valley of Elah, and set the battle in array against the Philistines.

3 And the Philistines stood on a mountain on the one side, and Israel stood on a mountain on the other side: and *there was* a valley between them.

4 And there went out a champion out of the camp of the Philistines, named Goliath, of Gath, whose height *was* six cubits and a span.

5 And *he had* an helmet of brass upon his head, and he *was* armed with a coat of mail; and the weight of the coat *was* five thousand shekels of brass.

6 And *he had* greaves of brass upon his legs, and a target of brass between his shoulders.

7 And the staff of his spear *was* like a weaver's beam; and his spear's head *weighed* six hundred shekels of iron: and one bearing a shield went before him.

8 And he stood and cried unto the armies of Israel, and said unto them, Why are ye come out to set *your* battle in array? *am* not I a Philistine, and ye servants to Saul? choose you a man for you, and let him come down to me.

9 If he be able to fight with me, and to kill me, then will we be your servants: but if I prevail against him, and kill him, then shall ye be our servants, and serve us.

10 And the Philistine said, I defy the armies of Israel this day; give me a man, that we may fight together.

11 When Saul and all Israel heard those words of the Philistine, they were dismayed, and greatly afraid.

12 Now David *was* the son of the Ephrathite of Beth-lehem-judah, whose name *was* Jesse; and he had eight sons: and the man went among men *for* an old man in the days of Saul.

13 And the three eldest sons of Jesse went *and* followed Saul to the battle: and the names of his three sons that went to the battle *were* Eliab the firstborn, and next unto him Abinadab, and the third Shammah.

14 And David *was* the youngest: and the three eldest followed Saul.

15 But David went and returned from Saul to feed his father's sheep at Beth-lehem.

16 And the Philistine drew near morning and evening, and presented himself forty days.

17 And Jesse said unto David his son, Take now for

thy brethren an ephah of this parched *corn*, and these ten loaves, and run to the camp to thy brethren;

18 And carry these ten cheeses unto the captain of *their* thousand, and look how thy brethren fare, and take their pledge.

19 Now Saul, and they, and all the men of Israel, *were* in the valley of Elah, fighting with the Philistines.

20 And David rose up early in the morning, and left the sheep with a keeper, and took, and went as Jesse had commanded him; and he came to the trench, as the host was going forth to the fight, and shouted for the battle.

21 For Israel and the Philistines had put the battle in array, army against army.

22 And David left his carriage in the hand of the keeper of the carriage, and ran into the army, and came and saluted his brethren.

23 And as he talked with them, behold, there came up the champion, the Philistine of Gath, Goliath by name, out of the armies of the Philistines, and spake according to the same words: and David heard *them*.

24 And all the men of Israel, when they saw the man, fled from him, and were sore afraid.

25 And the men of Israel said, Have ye seen this man that is come up? surely to defy Israel is he come up: and it shall be, *that* the man who killeth him, the king will enrich him with great riches, and will give him his daughter, and make his father's house free in Israel.

26 And David spake to the men that stood by him, saying, What shall be done to the man that killeth this Philistine, and taketh away the reproach from Israel? for who is this uncircumcised Philistine, that he should defy the armies of the living God?

27 And the people answered him after this manner, saying, So shall it be done to the man that killeth him.

28 And Eliab his eldest brother heard when he spake unto the men; and Eliab's anger was kindled against David, and he said, Why camest thou down hither? and with whom hast thou left those few sheep in the wilderness? I know thy pride, and the naughtiness of thine heart; for thou art come down that thou mightest see the battle.

29 And David said, What have I now done? Is *there* not a cause?

30 And he turned from him toward another, and spake after the same manner: and the people answered him again after the former manner.

31 And when the words were heard which David spake, they rehearsed *them* before Saul: and he sent for him.

32 And David said to Saul, Let no man's heart fail because of him; thy servant will go and fight with this Philistine.

33 And Saul said to David, Thou art not able to go against this Philistine to fight with him: for thou *art but* a youth, and he a man of war from his youth.

34 And David said unto Saul, Thy servant kept his father's sheep, and there came a lion, and a bear, and took a lamb out of the flock:

35 And I went out after him, and smote him, and delivered *it* out of his mouth: and when he arose against me, I caught *him* by his beard, and smote him, and slew him.

36 Thy servant slew both the lion and the bear: and this uncircumcised Philistine shall be as one of them,

seeing he hath defied the armies of the living God.

37 David said moreover, The LORD that delivered me out of the paw of the lion, and out of the paw of the bear, he will deliver me out of the hand of this Philistine. And Saul said unto David, Go, and the LORD be with thee.

38 And Saul armed David with his armour, and he put an helmet of brass upon his head; also he armed him with a coat of mail.

39 And David girded his sword upon his armour, and he assayed to go; for he had not proved *it*. And David said unto Saul, I cannot go with these; for I have not proved *them*. And David put them off him.

40 And he took his staff in his hand, and chose him five smooth stones out of the brook, and put them in a shepherd's bag which he had, even in a scrip; and his sling *was* in his hand: and he drew near to the Philistine.

41 And the Philistine came on and drew near unto David; and the man that bare the shield *went* before him.

42 And when the Philistine looked about, and saw David, he disdained him: for he was *but* a youth, and ruddy, and of a fair countenance.

43 And the Philistine said unto David, *Am* I a dog, that thou comest to me with staves? And the Philistine cursed David by his gods.

44 And the Philistine said to David, Come to me, and I will give thy flesh unto the fowls of the air, and to the beasts of the field.

45 Then said David to the Philistine, Thou comest to me with a sword, and with a spear, and with a shield: but I come to thee in the name of the LORD of hosts, the God of the armies of Israel, whom thou hast defied.

46 This day will the LORD deliver thee into mine hand: and I will smite thee, and take thine head from thee; and I will give the carcases of the host of the Philistines this day unto the fowls of the air, and to the wild beasts of the earth; that all the earth may know that there is a God in Israel.

47 And all this assembly shall know that the LORD saveth not with sword and spear: for the battle *is* the LORD'S, and he will give you into our hands.

48 And it came to pass, when the Philistine arose, and came and drew nigh to meet David, that David hasted, and ran toward the army to meet the Philistine.

49 And David put his hand in his bag, and took thence a stone, and slang *it*, and smote the Philistine in his forehead, that the stone sunk into his forehead; and he fell upon his face to the earth.

50 So David prevailed over the Philistine with a sling and with a stone, and smote the Philistine, and slew him; but *there was* no sword in the hand of David.

51 Therefore David ran, and stood upon the Philistine, and took his sword, and drew it out of the sheath thereof, and slew him, and cut off his head therewith. And when the Philistines saw their champion was dead, they fled.

52 And the men of Israel and of Judah arose, and shouted, and pursued the Philistines, until thou come to the valley, and to the gates of Ekron. And the wounded of the Philistines fell down by the way to Shaaraim, even unto Gath, and unto Ekron.

53 And the children of Israel returned from chasing after the Philistines, and they spoiled their tents.

54 And David took the head of the Philistine, and

brought it to Jerusalem; but he put his armour in his tent.

55 And when Saul saw David go forth against the Philistine, he said unto Abner, the captain of the host, Abner, whose son is this youth? And Abner said, *As* thy soul liveth, O king, I cannot tell.

56 And the king said, Enquire thou whose son the stripling *is*.

57 And as David returned from the slaughter of the Philistine, Abner took him, and brought him before Saul with the head of the Philistine in his hand.

58 And Saul said to him, Whose son *art* thou, *thou* young man? And David answered, I *am* the son of thy servant Jesse the Beth-lehemite.

The Conceited Man

LI CHAO DEVELOPED an interest in martial arts as a boy and had a full collection of weapons, such as the stick, broadsword, spear, sword and halberd.

In his spare time, Li Chao would invite friends and neighbours to spar with him. Since he had no teacher to instruct him, his martial arts skills were not very high, even though he possessed extraordinary physical strength.

One day when Li Chao and his friends were boxing, they heard someone shout, 'Your bravery is admirable, but it's a pity that your skills are so shallow.'

Hearing this, Li Chao could not help flaring up. He looked up and found a monk standing under a tree and smiling at him. Li Chao dashed over to the monk to punch him.

The monk calmly dodged his assault and stroked him

on the back. The blow sent him staggering to the ground. The monk laughed and said, 'You have a few more years of learning!' Li Chao blushed.

Li Chao got up and approached the monk. He bowed to him, taking him as his teacher. Moved by his sincerity, the monk readily agreed to receive him.

From then on, Li Chao was absorbed in learning and practising martial arts skills under the monk's instruction.

Three months later, Li Chao had made great progress and was often praised by his friends. He grew complacent again.

One day, the monk purposely asked him about his martial arts knowledge. Li Chao laughed and said, 'What the master knows, I know. What the master doesn't know, I also have a smattering of.'

When the monk asked Li Chao to display his skills. Li Chao showed everything to his master.

After that, Li Chao leapt over to the monk and said loudly, 'Master, your disciple's skill is perfect, isn't it?' The monk was silent.

Li Chao thought he had mastered every skill and began to grow lazy. Every day he would stay in bed until noon.

The monk tried to persuade him several times, but to no avail. Before long, the monk said good-bye to him and went away.

After the monk left, Li Chao issued an open challenge to show off his skills. More than ten days passed, but nobody took up the challenge. Li Chao was bored.

Li Chao set out for the provincial capital immediately upon hearing that there were many able fighters there. Li Chao wandered in the capital for several days, but to his disappointment, did not encounter a single worthy opponent.

One day, Li Chao found many people gathered at a crossroads. He joined the crowd and saw a girl of seventeen or so performing boxing. After the performance, the girl shouted to the audience, 'It's so boring to perform alone. Would anyone like to try his hand?'

Three people took up her challenge, but all were beaten by the girl. The audience praised her for her highly skilled martial arts.

Li Chao rushed over, intending to compete with the girl. Without saying a word, the girl met the attack of the fierce new challenger.

After the first round, the girl suddenly stopped and asked, 'Would you please tell me who your master is?'

'Why do you ask about my master?' said Li Chao. But as the girl kept questioning, he had to tell her his master's name.

Having heard the name, the girl raised her cupped hands and said, 'I admit my defeat. Let's stop here.' But Li Chao insisted on continuing. The girl had to go on fighting with Li Chao, who was eager to make a name for himself in the provincial capital by defeating his opponent.

The girl stopped again and said, 'We are of one family and it's quite enough to get the general idea with a simple competition.'

Thinking that girl might be scared, Li Chao punched her unawares, but the girl adroitly dodged his blow. Anxious to gain victory, Li Chao pressed forward steadily. The girl had no choice but to meet his attack.

With all of his strength, Li Chao tried to punch the

girl on the head. She lowered her head and chopped him on the leg. Li Chao tumbled to the ground. With her cupped hands before her chest, the girl apologised, 'Sorry for the offence,' and stalked off.

Li Chao was sent home by some of the onlookers. A month passed before the wound on his leg healed.

One day as Li Chao was sitting alone, the monk came in. Li Chao told the monk how he had taken a beating. The monk said, 'The girl is my fellow student. It's lucky you gave my name. Otherwise, your leg would have been broken.'

Taking the monk's hands, Li Chao said to him, 'Master, now I understand that however strong you are, there is always someone stronger.'

The Selfish Giant

EVERY AFTERNOON, AFTER school, some children played in the large, beautiful garden of a huge deserted castle. They rolled in the long, soft grass, hid behind the bushes covered with blossom and climbed trees where the birds sung sweetly. They were very happy there.

One afternoon they were playing hide-and-seek when they heard a great voice boom out. 'What are you doing in *my* garden?' it roared.

Trembling with fear, the children peered out of their hiding places to see a very angry giant. He had finally decided to come home after living for seven years with his friend, the Cornish ogre. 'I came back to my castle for some peace and quiet,' he thundered. 'I don't want to listen to a lot of children laughing and shouting. Get out of my garden – and don't come back.'

So the children ran away, as fast as their legs would carry them.

'This garden belongs to me, and nobody else,' the giant mumbled to himself. 'I shall make sure that nobody else can use it.' So he built a high wall all around it, with sharp iron spikes on top.

In the wall was a great iron gate, and on the gate the giant put a notice. 'KEEP OUT', it read. 'TRESPASSERS WILL BE PROSECUTED'. Every day the children poked their noses through the bars of the gate and looked longingly at the garden. Then, sadly, they wandered off to play on the hard, dusty road.

Soon the Winter came. Snow covered the ground with a thick white mantle and Frost painted the trees silver. The North Wind howled round the giant's castle and Hail pounded the window-panes. 'How I long for the Spring,' the giant sighed, as he sat huddled by the fire.

At last Spring came. The Snow and the Frost disappeared and the flowers pushed their heads up through the ground. The buds on the trees opened and the birds sang merrily – except in the giant's garden. There the Snow, the Frost, and the North Wind still danced through the bare branches of the trees.

'The Spring has refused to come to this garden,' they cried. 'At last we have a place where we can stay for ever.'

One morning the giant was lying awake in bed, feeling very sorry for himself, when he heard a blackbird singing. He leapt over to the window and beamed with pleasure. The Snow and the Frost had gone, and every tree had burst into blossom.

Every tree also held one of the children whom the giant

had frightened away. They had crept into the garden through a hole in the wall, and the Spring had rushed in after them. Only one child was still standing on the ground. He was a boy who was crying bitterly because he was too small to reach even the lowest branch of the smallest tree.

The giant was moved to pity. 'How selfish I have been,' he said to himself. 'Now I see why the Spring wouldn't come to my garden. I'll knock down the walls and turn it into a children's playground. But first I'll put that poor little boy on top of the tree.'

The giant crept down the stairs and into the garden, but when the children saw him they were so frightened they ran away again. Only the little boy, whose eyes were so full of tears that he could not see the giant coming, stayed where he was. As the Winter returned to the garden, the giant gently picked up the boy. 'There's no need to cry,' he murmured softly, and he placed the boy on top of the nearest tree. Immediately the tree burst into blossom. And the boy flung his arms around the giant's neck and kissed him.

When the children saw that the giant was kind and friendly, they came running back into the garden through the hole in the wall, followed by the Spring. The giant laughed happily and joined in their games, only stopping to knock down the walls with an axe. It was sunset before he realised that he had not seen the small boy for some time.

'Where is your little friend?' he asked anxiously. But the children did not know.

Every day after school the children came to play in the giant's beautiful garden. Every day the giant asked them the same question: 'Is the little boy with you today?' And every day the answer was the same:

'We don't know where to find him. The only time we've ever seen him was the day you knocked down the wall.'

The giant felt sad because he loved the little boy very much. Only the sight of the children playing made him happy again.

The years passed quickly and the giant grew old and weak. Soon he could no longer play with all the children.

One winter morning he was sitting by his bedroom window when he suddenly saw the most beautiful tree he had ever seen, standing in a corner of the garden. Its golden branches were covered with delicate white blossom and silver fruit – and underneath them stood the little boy.

'He's come back at last,' the giant said joyfully. Forgetting how weak his legs were, he rushed down the stairs and hurried across the garden. But as he reached the little boy his face became red with anger. 'Who has hurt you?' he cried. 'Why can I see the marks of nails on your hands and feet? Old and feeble as I am, I'll kill the people who have done this to you.'

Then the child smiled gently and said, 'Hush. Don't be angry, but come with me.'

'Who are you?' whispered the giant, falling to his knees.

'A long time ago you let me play in your garden,' the child replied. 'Now I want you to come and play in mine. It's called Paradise.'

That afternoon, when the children ran into the garden to play in the snow, they found the dead giant lying peacefully under a tree, all covered with white blossom.

Tseng and the Holy Man

TSENG WAS A handsome young man, well educated and talented. But he was also bumptious and boastful, as full of himself as a soap bubble. Everyone admired him, but nobody liked him. People smiled at him and rubbed their hands with pretended pleasure when they saw him – but only because they were afraid of what he might do when he became rich and powerful.

Rich and powerful! Tseng's ambition burned in his brain. The three things he wanted more than all the world were the dragon robes, red umbrella and brass-bound treasure-chest of a Minister of State.

One day Tseng and a group of other young men, out walking in the countryside, were caught in a storm. Rain-drops the size of duck-eggs pelted down; their sandals slithered and squelched on what had once been a dusty track; their clothes hung dark with rain. Even Tseng was soaked, for all his airs.

It was a case of finding shelter – anywhere, and soon. They didn't want to drown on dry land. They squelched through grey rain to the only house in sight: a broken-down hut of mud and straw. Its walls ran with water and wind roared in the eaves, but at least it had a roof.

Tseng pushed open the door and shouldered his way inside. The others crowded in after him. The hut was small and dark. A fire of dried dung flickered and spat. An old holy man sat cross-legged on the ground, still as a lizard. He took no notice of his guests. They fed and poked the fire, squeezed the wet from their clothes and sat down to warm the storm from their bones.

Soon, in the dark hut, the murmur of voices mingled with the thud of rain on the roof and the hiss of the fire. Tseng was drowsy, lost in a daydream of what he would do when he was rich and powerful. He had just, in his imagination, made his old gardener Prime Minister, when there was a jingle of harness from outside, a knock on the door, and in walked two heralds, dressed in the royal robes of the Emperor himself. One of them carried a red velvet cushion with a yellow scroll upon it; the other held a small umbrella to protect it from the rain.

The heralds bowed low to Tseng and handed him the scroll. It was nothing less than a letter from the Emperor's own secretary, inviting him to Peking to become a Minister of State. The heralds dressed him in dragon robes, gave him a red umbrella to keep off the rain, and led him to a fine house in the city, with a brass-bound treasure-chest in every room.

Tseng's job was an important one. He was an Official of the Second Grade, and was responsible for the promotion or dismissal of all the Officials below him, from the Third Grade down to the Ninth. He was a powerful man, and everyone wanted his favour. Presents of costly food arrived daily in his kitchens; his hall was thronged with flatterers; his treasure-chests bulged with gifts of coins, jewels and embroidered silk.

When Officials of the First or Second Grade came calling, Tseng would dress quickly in his finest robes and rush out to fawn and wheedle them, rubbing his hands and smiling his smile. But with underlings, Officials of the Third Grade and below, he was hard, cold as stone. One nod and a man was stripped of his power; one finger crooked and another man was thrashed without mercy. Power – and wealth! In a few years Tseng was richer than dreams, almost as powerful as the Emperor himself.

But power and wealth breed envy – especially if they grow from arrogance. As the years passed, other Ministers envied Tseng more and more; their envy curdled to hatred and their hatred into spite. Finally they sent a petition to the Emperor: all those who had once thronged to Tseng's door, who had fawned on him and called him 'Little Father', now accused him of treachery, cruelty and feeding fat on bribes.

The Emperor's answer was swift. The same two heralds (older and slower now) came to visit Tseng again. They brought another velvet cushion, another yellow scroll. Banishment, for life. They were followed by a whole army of removal-men, with mule-carts. All Tseng's treasure-chests, his wardrobes, his vessels and bales and crates, were stacked in the hall. Carts were piled high with bank-notes, jewels, silks, fabrics, caged humming-birds, wine-barrels and honey-jars. Curtains, carpets and bedspreads were folded and baled; a thousand pairs of shoes were wrapped in silk; lampshades, silver tea-caddies, ornaments of jet and jade, were crated and packed. The laden carts trundled away; the dust settled again on the cobble-stones; a detachment of squint-eyed, broken-down soldiers marched up in ragged step, to lead Tseng and his wife into exile, a thousand leagues away.

A thousand leagues! On foot, mile after endless mile. Mountains; marshes; deserts; stony tracks. Getting to exile was a lifetime's job. Or it would have been, except that on the first night of the second month, just as Tseng and his wife were settling down on a bed of desert stones, a band of robbers came down on them: leather breeches, shouts, moustaches and bristling swords. What use were the soldiers? None: fast as ferrets, they ran away.

'Spare me! Spare me!' cried Tseng, on his knees. 'I'm a poor man, an exile. Take my wife; spare me!'

'No!' thundered the robber chief. 'Look at our faces. We're your victims, the men you stripped and drove into exile. Now we want your head.'

'Dogs! said Tseng. 'Exiled I may be, but I am still an Official of the Second Grade, your superior. Bow and fawn!'

But the robbers crowded round, and the next thing Tseng heard was the plop of his own head as it hit the ground. Darkness loomed around him, and out of the velvet dark two blood-red devils appeared, chirping like monkeys. They took Tseng's hands in their scratchy paws and dragged him after them, chittering and squeaking with delight. As they went, a smooth stone path, blue as iron, opened up in front of them: the way to Hell.

They came to the city of the Emperor of Hell, and the hideous palace where he sits in state to judge the Dead. The devils flung Tseng on hands and knees and he crawled before the Emperor, whimpering for mercy. The Emperor turned to one of his Officials, who held a long grey scroll: the register of mankind and their deeds on earth.

'Name?' said the Emperor.

'Tseng,' answered the Official.

'His first crime?'

'He betrayed his friends.'

'The punishment: boiling oil.'

The Emperor gestured with his hollow hand, and all the ten thousand devils gathered in the hall shrieked with glee. They led Tseng to a brass cauldron two metres high and two across, filled with bubbling, smoking oil.

Tseng howled for mercy, but no one heard. Chuckling, the devils picked him up and dropped him into the oil. He splashed, sank and bobbed up again, like a fish deep-fried on the kitchen stove. He felt the burning oil seep into his body; it gnawed his bones till he screamed for death. But he was dead already, and all he could do was writhe and twist till the punishment was done. Then a devil fished him out with a boat-hook and dumped him down in front of the Emperor, floundering, gasping, sodden with oil.

'Tseng!' said the Emperor. 'Now for your second crime: injustice and insult. You used your position to harm others. Punishment: the hill of knives.'

The hill of knives! Compared to it, boiling oil was a pleasure, a soft delight. The devils took Tseng to a hillside studded with knives, set point-up in the ground like hedgehog's bristles. Bones and rags of flesh: the remains of previous victims. The devils tossed Tseng high in the air and let him fall on the points. Again. And again. Then they gathered the pieces in a basket and dumped him before the Emperor once more. Tseng groaned; he tried to hold his tattered flesh together; he begged for mercy.

'The third crime?'

'Embezzlement. He stole three million gold pieces.'

'Punishment?'

'He must drink the same amount.'

Three million gold pieces, melted down – a river, a searing waterfall. The devils thrust a funnel down Tseng's throat and began pouring in the molten gold. Gulping, twisting in agony, he drank and drank. When it was done and his punishments were over, the devils took him to a catherine wheel the size of a man. They fastened him to it and lit and fuse. Round the wheel fizzed, faster and faster. Light and darkness blurred together, burning Tseng's eyes. His screamed and screamed.

Well, it was a dream. Of course it was a dream. Tseng woke to find his companions shaking him, trying to snatch him from his nightmare. He sat up and shook his head. The holy man's lizard-eyes were open, and a smile flickered on his papery lips. 'Tseng, Tseng,' he said in a voice like bank-notes blown on a summer breeze, ' Have you learned? Do you know your future now?'

Tseng bowed his head. Outside, the rain was finished; the sun shone; crickets chirped; the green ground steamed. He went home an altered man. Ambition is not an evil thing; but evil ambition always destroys a man. Be honest and true: for good men, even in the volcano's heart, a lily will always grow. So Tseng was saved from ambition; he lived a long, uneventful life, honest and true, loved by all his friends; and when he died the devils carried him to happiness, the true reward for loyalty.

And the holy man? He waited, cross-legged in his hut like a lizard in a wall, to set the next visitor's feet on the path of truth.

Gypsies Who All But Cheated Themselves

THERE WERE ONCE two brother gypsies who lived by craft and guile. They owned a jet-black stallion – no ordinary steed. As the brothers went about their business, that horse could sense danger a mile off. If it stamped the ground, that spelt trouble. So whenever they were on a job, they left the stallion on the road and kept close watch on it.

One time they thought to rob a merchant, left their stallion close by, and crept towards a barn. Unfortunately for them, a massive old padlock hung from the barn door, and there was no way in.

'Know what, brother?' whispered one, 'Let's dig a tunnel beneath the door.'

The tunnel was duly dug and, while one crawled into the barn, the other stood guard, ready to receive the booty.

Now, good folk, you should know that every barn has its goblin. You don't know what a goblin is? Well, he can take any form – human, bird or animal – and he lives in the farmyard protecting the animals. If he takes to a horse, fancies its colour or something else, he'll protect it himself, brushing its mane and coat until they gleam, and its eyes are bright and keen. The goblin always pets his favourites, gives them fond pats. And you don't have to feed such animals - their bellies are full without your fodder.

But if he takes a dislike to any beast, sell it forthwith or he'll drive it round the yard, torment it until tears roll down its muzzle. He might even set to tickling the poor beasts, and that will make them mad, foam at the mouth, choke and die.

You have to respect the goblin, bring him bread and salt – he adores respect. Of an evening, as the sun goes down, you must go into the yard to pay your respects, say this, that and the other – 'Dear Master Goblin,' 'regards to your children,' 'do let my horse come quietly' – and you'll have bread and salt a'plenty. And don't forget to bow three times…

So now the goblin watched crossly as the gypsy crawled into the barn and set to steal a sheep.

'Hey gypsy!' the goblin shrieked in rage, 'leave that sheep be; if you touch a hair on its back I'll skin you alive.'

And they came to blows. Meanwhile the stallion on the road was snorting and stamping as it sensed the danger.

After some time the gypsy emerged from the barn empty-handed – the goblin had got the better of him.

65

'I put up a fight,' he told his brother, 'but how can you beat a goblin? He tossed me into the hayloft, and as I slid down he threw me into the food trough; next he hoisted me onto the ram's horns. He shook me and twisted me, I tell you I was lucky to escape.'

'Listen, brother,' said the other, 'my wife tells me they've just slaughtered a hog here, ready for the holiday. Surely the goblin won't be guarding a dead hog.'

'You're right; let's steal the hog.'

Both glanced round at their horse – it seemed to be standing quietly now. So they crept towards the outhouse, right by the farmhouse. By now it was so dark you could poke out your eye in the gloom. The outhouse was even worse. At last their fumbling fingers felt the dead carcass of the hog, and they quickly heaved it on to their shoulders and made off with it. Dropping it into their cart and covering it up with sacking, they made off post-haste.

'Phew!' sighed one, 'That's some hog; we barely carried it between us.'

'I'm famished after that tussle with the goblin,' said the other. 'I could do with some roast pork. Let's get a fire going now and fry us some pig.'

'Hold on, brother, we'd better be well clear of the village first. Let's wait until we come home and have a good feast there.'

By the time they reached home it was quite light, and a crowd of gypsies came out to meet them.

'How did it go, lads?'

'See for yourselves, there's a hog in the cart under the sacking. Let's shift it indoors.'

Two strong gypsies went over to the cart, drew aside the sacking and froze in their tracks.

'What's this?' they cried.

Rushing to the cart, the brothers looked in and... could not believe their eyes. A dead man lay there, cold and stiff!

What were they to do? It had to be disposed of before the villagers came searching. So they carried it indoors, lay it on the stove, and sat down to think, not daring to glance towards the dead man.

As they were discussing what to do, they suddenly heard a noise from the stove. Staring in disbelief, they saw first an arm and then a leg move. Next one eye opened followed by the second, and both eyes started round the room.

Gypsies don't scare easily, that's well known, but there was fear now in the room. It dawned on the brothers that the fellow must have been dead drunk and the villagers had taken him for dead, dumping him in his own shed. And they had picked up his body in the dark! Having got over their fear they wondered how they might somehow profit from this error.

Before their eyes the dead man slowly sat up and spoke, 'Where I am?'

'You're in hell,' the gypsies told him. 'We're demons and we're just preparing a pot to roast you in.'

'Oh, please don't, dear demons,' wailed the man, 'I'll make it worth your while...'

'Why, do you want to go back to earth?'

'I do, I do, dear demons, there's nothing I wouldn't give.'

'Right, let's strike a bargain: we'll take you home, and you reward us well.

The deal was struck. The man was wrapped up again, placed in the cart and driven back to the village. By now the loss had been discovered, and the dead man's household was yelling and wailing. Then all of a sudden the door burst open and in came the gypsies carrying the dead body.

'You bandits, grave-robbers!' yelled the peasants. 'You can't even leave the dead in peace!'

'Hold your shouting and take a look,' the gypsies said.

As the sacking was drawn back, the 'dead' man sat up. What a hullabaloo! Some fainted clean away; but the 'dead' master of the house rewarded the gypsy demons well, giving them the very sheep they had earlier tried to steal.

'That's for delivering me from Hell,' he said.

So you see, wonders abound...if you play your cards right!

The Gypsy Who Did Not Keep His Word

A GYPSY ONCE WENT off horse-stealing, leaving his family behind within the gypsy camp. They waited one day, a second and a third, but there was no sign or news. Now what? In her alarm, the wife roused the whole gypsy band to go in search. They searched here and there without success, finally deciding that he was dead.

In his memory they held a funeral service, his wife poured out her tears and…in the passing of time, cast him out of mind. That's life, isn't it?

But this is the strange story of his disappearance.

'In the depths of night he pushed on through the forest and emerged into a glade where he spied a steed of stunning beauty. It stood there quietly grazing. Its mane was long, its tail reached to the ground, and white sparks flew from beneath its hoofs. In a single bound it cleared the entire glade.

69

How the gypsy longed to catch that steed. Yet every time he approached it darted aside and neighed so hard it made the ground shake. Finally, it galloped off, leaving the gypsy standing and staring. And not a little ashamed.

'I'm no novice at catching horses,' he groaned, 'yet that horse escaped me. Just wait; I'll tame it yet.'

And he took up the chase. That day went by, another dawned, and at last the hoof marks brought him to the entrance of a rocky cave. Without hesitation, he went inside and followed the tunnel down, down in the bowels of the earth. And he found himself in the underground realm of serpents.

The chief Serpent in that realm was a huge twelve-headed monster who made everyone in his power obey him. As soon as he saw the gypsy he flew at him, hissing in an awesome voice, 'How dare you enter my kingdom!'

The gypsy tried not to display his fear. 'When gypsies see fine steeds,' he said, 'they give chase wherever the trail leads. So it is; that's how I came here.'

'There is no return for you, gypsy,' hissed the Serpent. 'Now you must make your choice: be my slave or die.'

Well, who chooses death?

So the gypsy began to work for the Serpent and was made to groom the enchanted steeds. That suited him well.

One year passed, another and a third. And the busy gypsy earned the admiration of the Serpent, so well did he tend the magic steeds. And one day the Serpent summoned him and said, 'What do you say to going home?'

For three whole years the gypsy had thought of nothing else but gazing on his wife and children again. The Serpent's words cheered him no end.

'I'll let you go, gypsy, since you've served me well. But there's one condition: no one must learn of where you have been. If you break that vow your fate is sealed.'

Striking the ground with its tail, the Serpent gave a whistle and all the other serpents formed a ball about the gypsy; as the earth opened up the ball of tangled snakes began to roll, with the gypsy caught inside it. It rolled and rolled until it reached the daylight.

'Climb out,' ordered the twelve-headed Serpent.

And the gypsy crawled out into the light of day, stared about him blinking, and did not even notice the ball of snakes disappearing into the ground.

'Mind you keep your vow,' hissed the Serpent King.

'On the lives of my wife and children, I shall not tell!' he swore.

And off he ran home. When he appeared, of course, the gypsies thought it must be a ghost. Had he returned from the dead? But he convinced them he was alive and well, and naturally his wife and children were overjoyed.

'Where have you been, dear husband?' his wife asked once they were inside their tent. 'How did you disappear for so long? Do tell us.'

He was so happy to be back with his family that a mist seemed to cloud his mind, and he forgot his vow. His wife and children listened open-mouthed as he told the story of his adventures underground. Only at the end did he realise what he had done…

'Oh, *Devaley*!' he cried. 'God, what have I done?'

With a strangled cry, he fell to the ground and began to twist and turn in torment. He twisted, squirmed, writhed…and turned into a venomous snake. Then, setting upon his wife and children, he bit each one in turn and his poison struck them down: they fell beside him on the ground, writhing in pain.

Next morning when the gypsies glanced into the tent they saw the wife and children lying cold and dead. And across their lifeless bodies crawled a hissing snake.

The Father

THE MAN I am going to tell you about in this story was the most powerful in his parish. His name was Tor Overas. One day he was standing in the vicar's office; he was tall and his mood was serious, 'I have a son,' he said, 'and I want you to christen him.'

'What shall you call him?'

'Finn, it was my father's name.'

'And the godparents?'

Tor gave the priest the names of two of his relatives; they were both well-off and well-respected.

'That's that then,' said the vicar. 'Are there any other details?'

The farmer paused and then said, 'I want a private christening.'

'That will mean doing it on a weekday, then?'

'Yes, next Saturday at twelve noon.'

'You are sure?'

'Yes, quite sure.'

'Is there anything else you wish to say to me?' asked the vicar.

'No, that's all,' and the farmer put on his hat and made as if to leave. The vicar rose from his desk and took the farmer by the hand and said, 'Pray to God that the boy will be a blessing to you.'

Sixteen years later Tor came to the vicar's office. 'You look well,' said the vicar.

'I haven't a care in the world.'

The vicar said nothing. After a while he asked Tor why he had come to see him.

'I'm here to talk about my son's confirmation. He's an intelligent lad and I'd like you to perform the ceremony tomorrow morning. But I won't pay you until you tell me which row he will be sitting in.'

'He will be number one in the first row.'

'Excellent. Here's your money.' And he placed ten large coins on the vicar's table.

'Will that be all, then?'

'Yes, that's all.' And Tor left.

Eight years passed. Then one day the vicar heard a hubbub outside his door; several men stood there and Tor was at the front. The vicar recognised him at once. 'My goodness,' he said, 'so many people.'

'I am here to make an announcement on my son's behalf: he is to marry Karen Storlien, the daughter of Gudmund here.'

'She is the richest girl in the parish,' observed the vicar.

'So they say,' said Tor, drawing his hand over his brow. For a moment the vicar remained silent. Then he took up his pen and wrote the details of the marriage in the official book and the two men added their signatures. Tor put three large coins on the vicar's table.

'It only costs one,' said the vicar.

'I know, but he is my only son and I want the best.'

The vicar took the money and looked up at Tor, 'This is the third time you have come to me about your son's business.'

'Yes, and the last. My responsibilities to him are over now.' Tor pocketed his wallet, turned and said his farewells. The other men followed slowly after him.

Two weeks later Tor and his son were rowing across the lake to finalise the details of the wedding. The weather was perfect and the lake was like a mirror. 'This seat is really uncomfortable,' said the son and stood up to see what was wrong. As he turned around, he lost his footing and fell backwards with a scream into the lake. 'Grab the oars,' shouted Tor and reached out towards him. His son flailed and then he seemed to freeze. 'Hold on,' begged Tor as he rowed towards him. Then suddenly his son made one last effort to reach the boat, looked deep into his father's eyes and disappeared under the water.

Tor could not believe his eyes. He held the boat steady at the very point his son had gone under, waiting for him to resurface. A few bubbles came up, followed by one large bubble which burst, and then nothing. The lake was like a mirror once more.

For three days and three nights people observed Tor

rowing round and round at the spot where his son had drowned. He neither ate nor slept. Finally he found his son and he carried him home to his farm.

It was a year later that the vicar heard a sound outside his door. He opened up and a tall man entered. He was very thin and had white hair; he had a terrible stoop. The vicar looked at him for a long time and finally recognised him as Tor, 'What brings you here so late?'

'Yes it's late. I'm here too late.' Tor sat down. The vicar joined him. Nothing was said for a little while. Then Tor said, 'I have something that I would like you to give to the poor; use it as a fund for needy people and set it up in my son's name.' He rose and put a sack of coins on the table. Then he sat down again. The vicar looked in the sack, 'There's an awful lot of money here.'

'I sold my farm today.'

They sat in silence for some minutes. After some time the vicar asked, 'What will you do with yourself, Tor?'

'Something better,' he replied. And there they sat, quietly: Tor staring at the floor; the vicar looking at Tor. And there they sat till it was quite dark. 'I think,' said the vicar slowly and solemnly, 'I think that your son has finally been a blessing to you.'

'Yes. Yes, I think so too,' said Tor, and he looked up, tears running down his face like rain.

The Fisherman

T HERE WAS A young fisherman from Helgeland whose name was Isak.

One day he was out in the fjord fishing for halibut when he felt something heavy on his line. He reeled it in and discovered that he had caught a fisherman's boot. 'Strange,' he said, staring at his catch. The boot looked just like the type his brother was wearing when he was lost in the fjord during a terrible storm. There was something in the boot but he did not dare look what it was.

And he did not know what to do with his gruesome find.

He could not take it home. It would scare the living daylights out of his mother. But he could not bring himself to throw it back.

He decided to take the boot to the local vicar and ask him to give it a proper burial.

'I can't bury a fisherman's boot,' said the vicar.

'No, I suppose not.'

But Isak wanted to know how much of a person there had to be before it could have a proper burial.

'I don't know the answer,' said the vicar. 'It's not a tooth or a finger or a lock of hair. However, there should be enough left for me to know that it once had a soul. And a toenail at the bottom of a boot is, quite frankly, too little.

Despite the vicar's ruling, Isak decided to bury the boot in the graveyard anyway. He did it discreetly, then left. He felt he had done the best he could. Surely it was better to place something belonging to his dead brother in hallowed ground than to throw the boot back out to sea?

It was late autumn when he was out after cod and brought up a leather belt. He recognised it immediately: it was his brother's.

The buckle had been tarnished by the sea. He remembered quite clearly how his brother had fashioned the leather, which they had got from their old horse when it had died. They had bought the buckle together over at the general stores one Saturday. They had had a bit to drink and had flirted with the girls who made the sails down by the quay.

He kept quiet about the belt and hid it in his room. He did not want to cause his mother any pain by telling her about it.

As the winter drew on he began to think more and more about what the vicar had said.

He began to worry about how he would react if he reeled in another boot or some bone that the fish had been gnawing at.

And so he became scared of going out to fish in the fjord. Yet he could not stop himself going back to the places where he had found his brother's remains. He desperately wanted to find enough of his brother so that the vicar could tell that the soul had been there; then the vicar could perform the ceremony.

And then he began to have nightmares.

The door would fly open in the middle of the night and a cold wind stinking of seaweed would blow in and he sensed his brother was in the room, moaning and screaming in pain, howling for his lost foot. Being without it was agony.

Isak could hardly work now. He could barely lift a hand; he just stared into the middle distance. He felt that the burden of burying his brother's boot in the cemetery was finally driving him crazy.

Yet he could not throw the boot back in the water.

All he wanted was for his brother to get a decent burial. He could not bear the thought of his corpse lying out there at the bottom of the fjord being messed about by whatever was down there.

Finally he plucked up the courage to start fishing again. At first he fished close in to land but he did not have much success. So he took his boat further out to try his luck there.

It was early evening and he was preparing his first cast. He got hold of the lead weight and threw it into the water. The line with the fifty baited hooks fairly flew after it but the last hook caught his eye as it went past, tore the eyeball from the socket and down it went to the bottom of the fjord.

There was no point in looking for it; so he rowed back home.

That night he lay in bed, a bandage over his eye. He was in great pain and could not sleep. Everything seemed to go black and he thought he must be the most forlorn person in the world.

Then a strange event occurred: he felt as if he was transported to the bottom of the sea. As he looked round, he noticed how the fish flitted about near the baited hooks. When they took the bait, they struggled like mad to be free: first a cod, next a haddock. Then a small shark appeared, looked closely at the bait, and took it. While all this was going on, Isak realised what he had really been looking at: it was the remains of a body; he could see the leather-clad back quite clearly; it was jammed under a five-pronged anchor.

As he was staring at what was left of his brother, a large fish approached the bait. Then everything went dark.

'You must let me go in the morning,' said the large fish. 'The hook is agony, agony. By the way, only fish at night when the tide is on the turn – it's the only time you'll catch anything.'

Next day Isak went down to the cemetery and picked up a piece of broken gravestone to use as a weight for his fishing line. That evening as the tide turned, he set his line.

Straight away he got a bite and hauled in the line: there was the five-pronged anchor with the leather coat on it. Looking more closely, he saw the remains of an arm in the sleeve. That was all; the fish had obviously had the rest.

He took his grim catch to the vicar.

'You really expect me to give the last rites to a sodden old bit of leather?'

'Don't forget the boot as well.'

'Flotsam and jetsam is not enough,' thundered the vicar.

Isak looked the vicar straight in the eye. 'The burden of my brother's boot has been hard enough to bear. I can't face the arm as well.'

'And I am not prepared to waste a patch of hallowed ground on a load of rubbish!' Now the vicar was angry.

'No, I suppose not.' And with that Isak went home.

He could not relax. The weight of his dead brother preyed on his mind. At night he saw that same big fish swimming sadly round in the same slow circle. It was almost as though there was an invisible net surrounding it. And he stared and stared at it until his blind eye ached with the pain. Then a large octopus drenched everything with foul, dark ink; and darkness descended.

One evening he went out in his boat and let the current take it out towards a group of little islands. There the boat came to a standstill and everything became quiet. Not a sound was to be heard. All of a sudden a huge bubble burst by the side of the boat.

Isak saw something and he understood what it meant.

'The vicar will be carrying out a funeral soon,' he said to himself.

From that moment on, Isak got a reputation for having psychic powers. He could predict where the best places to fish would be, and, when people asked him how he knew, he replied, 'It's my brother who gives me the information.'

And then came the day when the vicar had to go out into the fjord to do his annual blessing of the water. Isak was one of the men who rowed the vicar out into the fjord. In the distance there was a rumble of thunder as the vicar completed his thanksgiving.

'The weather looks as if it's on the turn,' said the vicar. 'Best we get back.'

Just as they started on the return journey, a storm hit them. The snow swirled about and the sea seemed as big as houses. Then one of the timbers cracked and water poured into the boat and everyone screamed that they were going to sink.

'Be calm. We'll make it,' said Isak grimly as he held fast to the rudder.

The moon broke through the cloud cover and shone on the hole in the boat. A strange figure was there, baling out the water for all he was worth.

'Who's that man?' said the vicar. 'I don't understand. He's baling out water with a fisherman's boot. His legs are bare and ... his leather jacket seems empty.'

'You've seen him before,' said Isak.

At this the vicar lost his patience. 'I command you by the hand of God to leave this boat, unholy spirit.'

'Fine,' said Isak, 'but can you command the water to stop pouring in through that hole?'

The vicar paused. 'The man does seem to have

superhuman power and at this moment we do have great need of such a man. It is no crime to help one of God's servants across a stormy sea. So, what do you require in return for saving us?'

The wind howled.

'Just a few shovels full of earth placed on a sailor's boot and a leather sleeve,' said Isak.

'I grant you your blessing. You'll get your proper burial.'

No sooner had the vicar uttered these words than a huge wave seemed to pick the vicar's boat up and shoot it towards dry land, where it came to rest with a thud, breaking the mast clean in two.

The Pardoner's Tale

Now, ladies and gentlemen I'll tell you my tale.

It's about three drunken louts
Who, long before the first church bell had sounded,
Were sitting drinking in a tavern;
And as they sat there, they heard a clinking noise out-
side:
A corpse was being taken for burial.

So one of these lads called over the serving boy and
said,
'You see that funeral procession outside
Go and ask what happened.
And make sure you find out the exact name
Of the poor bloke that died.'

'Sir,' said the boy, 'I don't need to.
I found that out two hours before you arrived.

The Pardoner's Tale
(original version)

Thise riotóurės thre of whiche I tellė,
Long erst er primė rong of any bellė,
Were set hem in a taverne for to drynkė;
And as they sat they herde a bellė clynkė
Biforn a cors, was caried to his gravė.

That oon of hem gan callen to his knavė,
'Go bet,' quod he, 'and axė redilý
What cors is this that passeth heer forbý,
And looke that thou reportė his namė weel.'

'Sire,' quod this boy, 'it nedeth neveradeel;
It was me toold er ye cam heer two hourės.

He was, in fact, an old mate of yours.
Killed he was, like a bolt out of the blue;
Just sitting on that bench right there having a drink or
    two.
You see, he was visited by a cunning thief, who goes
    by the name of Death.
The villain's going about these parts slaughtering folk.
He took his spear to your mate and ripped his heart in
    two.
Then he left without further ado.
He's finished off many a thousand like this.
I tell you, sir, if you should happen to meet him,
Have your wits about you,
'Cause he plays dirty.
So watch out, you can meet Death anywhere.
That's what my old mother taught me, and I stick by
    it.'

'By God,' said the landlord of the tavern,
'The lad's right, I mean, this twelve months
He's virtually wiped out a whole village, not a mile
    from here.
All dead; men, women, children and workers, the lot.
It's my opinion that he lives near that village.
But take heed and be wary
Of crossing the likes of him.'

'Good God,' said one of the louts, 'He can't be that
    dangerous, I don't believe it.
No, I'll face him – I'll search high and low.
I swear to this on the bones of the Lord our God.
Listen lads, we're all for one, aren't we?
Let's make a pact and shake hands on it.

He was, pardee, an old feláwe of yourès,
And sodeynly he was yslayn tonyght,
Fordronke, as he sat on his bench uprìght.
Ther cam a privee heef, men tclepeth Deeth,
That in this contree al the peple sleeth,
And with his spere he smoot his herte atwo,
And wente his wey withouten wordès mo.
He hath a thousand slayn this pestiléncè;
And, maister, er ye come in his preséncè,
Me thynketh that it werè necessárie
For to be war of swich an adversárie.
Beth redy for to meete hym everemoorè:
Thus taughtè me my dame: I sey namoorè.'

'By Seintè Marie!' seyde this tavernér,
'The child seith sooth, for he hath slayn this yeer,
Henne over a mile, withinne a greet villágè,
Bothe man and womman, child, and hyne, and page;
I trowe his habitacióun be therè.
To been avysèd greet wysdom it werè,
Er that he dide a man a dishonóur.'

'Ye, Goddès armès!' quod this riotóur,
'Is it swich peril with hym for to meetè?
I shal hym seke by wey and eek by stretè,
I make avow to Goddès dignè bonès!
Herkneth, feláwès, we thre been al onès:
Lat ech of us holde up his hand til oother,

Aye, we'll be like blood brothers
And we'll find this traitor Death and do him in.
We'll have him. I mean, he's a mass murderer.
We'll do it before it gets dark.'

And there and then they promised
To live and die for each other
Just as if they were true brothers.
So off they went in a drunken rage
And made their way towards the desolate village
That the landlord had talked about earlier.
They cussed and swore so much
That it had the angels weeping in heaven.
Still, on they trudged, quite certain that Death would
    die,
If they could lay their hands on Him.

Well, they hadn't gone more than half-a-mile
And were just about to cross a stile
When they met an ancient, poor-looking character.

The old man greeted them humbly, 'God be with you,
    gents.'

Now the ring-leader of the louts approached him, 'By
    heck, you're an ugly old goat.
No wonder you're all muffled up – pity you didn't
    cover your face.
My God but you're old – I'm surprised you're alive.'

The old man turned and looked this lout straight in
    the eye,
'You know, if I walked to Hell and back,
Through city, town and village

And ech of us bicomen otheres brother,
And we wol sleen this falsė traytour Deeth –
He shal be slayn, he that so manye sleeth,
By Goddės dignitee, er it be nyght!'

Togidres han thise thre hir trouthės plight
To lyve and dyėn ech of hem for oother,
As though he were his owene yborė brother.
And up they stirte and dronken in this ragė,
And forth they goon towardės that villágė
Of which the taverner hadde spoke biforn,
And many a grisly ooth thanne han they sworn,
And Cristės blessėd body they to-rentė –
Deeth shal be deed, if that they may hym hentė!

Whan they han goon nat fully half a milė,
Right as they wolde han troden over a stilė,
An oold man and a povrė with hem mette.

This oldė man ful mekėly hem grettė,
And seydė thus, 'Now, lordės, God yow see!'

The proudeste of thise riotóurės three
Answérde agayn, 'What, carl with sory gracė!
Why artow al forwrappėd, save thy facė?
Why lyvestow so longe in so greet agė?'

This oldė man gan looke in his viságė,
And seydė thus, 'For I ne kan nat fyndė
A man, though that I walkėd into Yndė,
Neither in citee nor in no villágė,

I am quite certain that I would meet nobody
Who would willingly swap their youth for my old age
And so I must keep the years I have still.
Well, as long as it's God's will.
Not even Death himself – no, not even Death will take
    my life.
And so it is my lot to wander through the land like a
    wretched prisoner…
…So God be with you, wherever you may roam.
For I must continue on my journey.'

'Not so fast, old goat, not so fast,'
Said another of these louts. 'I heard you mention the
    name of that villain, Death.
The one who's going round the country killing all our
    mates.
I get the feeling that you're one of his spies,
So tell us where he is, or pay for it with your life.
By God, I think I'm right, you're one of his agents
Sent out to kill us young-bloods, you filthy, lying
    cheater.'

'Now wait, young sirs,' said the old man. 'If you are
    so keen
To find Death, then follow this crooked path;
You see I came from Death; he was in the wood up
    there,
Under a tree, he'll still be there, I'm sure.
He's not a one to run away from the likes of you.
Do you see that great oak, that's where he'll be.
Now, God be with you again,
And may He mend your ways' – these were the old
    man's parting words.

That woldė chaunge his youthė for myn agė;
And therfore moot I han myn agė stillė,
As longė tyme as it is Goddės willė.
Ne Deeth, allas! ne wol nat han my lyf;
Thus walke I lyk a restėlees kaitýf,
And God be with yow, where ye go or rydė!
I moote go thider as I have to go.'

'Nay, oldė cherl, by God, thou shalt nat so,'
Seydė this oother hasardour anon,
'Thou partest nat so lightly, by Seint John!
Thou spak right now of thilkė traytour Deeth,
That in this contree alle oure freendės sleeth.
Have heer my trouthe, as thou art his espýė,
Telle where he is, or thou shalt it abýė,
By God and by the hooly sacremént!
For soothly thou art oon of his assent
To sleen us yongė folk, thou falsė theef!'

'Now, sires,' quod he, 'if that ye be so leef
To fyndė Deeth, turne up this crokėd wey;
For in that grove I laftė hym, by my fey,
Under a tree, and there he wole abydė;
Noght for youre boost he wole him nothyng hydė.
Se ye that ook? Right there ye shal hym fyndė.
God savė yow that boghte agayn mankyndė,
And yow amende!' Thus seyde this oldė man;

The louts just ran on, not listening,
Until they came to the oak tree and there they found
A massive pile of newly-struck gold florins
Nearly half-a-ton in weight, they reckoned.
And so their search for Death stopped there and then;
They only had eyes for their treasure.
The golden florins shone so bright –
They just sat and stared at their precious hoard.

Now the nastiest of the thugs was the first to speak,
'Brothers,' he said, 'listen carefully.
Now I'm a canny lad, even though I act the fool at
    times
And I reckon that Lady Luck has smiled on us with
    this gold.
And now we can live a life of leisure.
Easy come, easy go – we'll have no trouble spending
    it.
By God, I can't believe the luck we've had today.
If only we could sneak the gold away
To my house, or to yours –
If we manage that the gold is ours – make no mistake;
Now that would be a real cause for celebration.
But the problem is, we can't take it home by daylight
Folks will think we've stolen it;
Then we'll end up being hanged for what's rightfully
    ours.
No, the gold must be smuggled in under the cover of
    darkness.
Aye, and as cunningly and as quietly as possible.
So here's my plan – let's draw straws.
And he who gets the longest, lucky lad,

And everich of thise riotóurės ran
Til he cam to that tree, and ther they foundė
Of floryns fyne of gold ycoynėd roundė
Wel ny an eightė busshels, as hem thoughtė.
No lenger thannė after Deeth they soughtė,
But ech of hem so glad was of that sightė,
For that the floryns been so faire and brightė,
That doun they sette hem by this precious hoord.

The worste of hem, he spak the firstė word.
'Bretheren,' quod he, 'taak kepė what I seye;
My wit is greet, though that I bourde and pleyė.
This tresor hath Fortúne unto us yiven,
In myrthe and joliftee oure lyf to lyven,
And lightly as it comth, so wol we spendė.
Ey, Goddės precious dignitee! who wendė
Today that we sholde han so fair a gracė?
But myghte this gold be caried fro this placė
Hoom to myn hous, or ellės unto yourės –
For wel ye woot that al this gold is ourės –
Thanne werė we in heigh felicitée!
But trewėly, by daye it may nat bee:
Men woldė seyn that we were thevės strongė,
And for oure owenė tresor doon us hongė.
This tresor moste ycaried be by nyghtė
As wisely and as slyly as it myghtė.
Wherfore I rede that cut among us allė
Be drawe, and lat se wher the cut wol fallė;
And he that hath the cut with hertė blithė

93

Will nip back into town, straight away
To get some bread and wine in –
But be careful not to attract attention.
Now the other two will stay here, in hiding,
To guard our treasure – and if the other one's quick
    about it,
As soon as it gets dark we can smuggle the treasure
    back,
To a safe place that we all agree upon.'

So he put three straws in his fist
And told them to draw and then compare the straws.
It was the youngest of the three who won
And immediately he set off on his trek back to town.

Now no sooner had he gone
Than one spoke to the other, 'You know you swore to
    be my brother
Well you're going to find why that was a good move,
    my son.
Of course you know that our other "brother" has
    gone;
And here we are with all this wealth in gold,
Which we are going to split three ways.
Now, say I could fix it
That this here gold be split two ways,
You would be inclined to say that I'd done you a good
    turn, right?'

So the other thug said, 'I can't see how you're going to
    fix it.

Shal rennè to the towne, and that ful swithè,
And brynge us breed and wyn ful privèlý.
And two of us shul kepen subtillý
This tresor wel; and if he wol nat tarie,
Whan it is nyght we wol this tresor carie
By oon assent, where as us thynketh best.'

That oon of hem the cut broghte in his fest,
And bad hem drawe, and looke where it wol fallè;
And it fil on the yongeste of hem allè,
And forth toward the toun he wente anon.

And also soone as that he was agon,
That oon of hem spak thus unto that oother:
'Thou knowest wel thou art my sworè brother;
Thy profit wol I tellè thee anon.
Thou woost wel that oure felawe is agon,
And heere is gold, and that ful greet plentée,
That shal departed been among us thre.
But nathèlees, if I kan shape it so
That it departed were among us two,
Hadde I nat doon a freendès torn to thee?'

That oother answèrde, 'I noot hou that may be;

Our mate knows damn well that we two are guarding
    the gold.
So what's the plan? What do we say?
How do we convince him when he gets back?'

'First, let's get things straight.
This is our secret, all right?' said the first young thug.
'And now a few words about the tactics
Of the cunning plan.'
'Fair enough,' his mate nodded, 'don't worry.
We'll keep this strictly between ourselves.'

'Good, now, you don't need me to tell you
That two blokes are stronger than one.
So, as soon as he gets back,
Jump on him, you know, like its some wrestling game
And while you're struggling, I'll run him through with
    my knife,
And have your dagger ready so you can do the same.
And so, my old mate, now you see
How this here gold will be split between you and me.
And we can satisfy our wildest desires,
And gamble and drink whenever we choose.

And so these two villains agreed
To kill the third.

The young lad, who went to town
Kept conjuring up in his mind's eye
The sheer beauty of the golden florins.
'O Lord,' he said to himself, 'if only there was a way
For me to have this treasure for my own.
No one in the whole wide world
Would be a happier man.'

He woot wel that the gold is with us tweyė;
What shal we doon? What shal we to hym seyė?'

'Shal it be conseil?' seyde the firstė shrewė,
'And I shal tellen in a wordės fewė
What we shal doon, and brynge it wel aboutė.'
'I grauntė,' quod that oother, 'out of doute,
That by my trouthe I wol thee nat biwreyė.'

'Now,' quod the firste, 'thou woost wel we be tweyė,
And two of us shul strenger be than oon.
Looke whan that he is set, thou right anoon
Aryse, as though thou woldest with hym pleyė,
And I shal ryve hym thurgh the sydės tweyė
Whil that thou strogelest with hym as in gamė,
And with thy daggere looke thou do the samė;
And thanne shal al this gold departed be,
My deerė freend, bitwixen me and thee.
Thanne may we bothe oure lustės all fulfillė,
And pleye at dees right at oure owenė willė.'

And thus acorded been thise shrewės tweyė
To sleen the thridde, as ye han herd me seyė.

This yongeste, which that wentė to the toun,
Ful ofte in herte he rolleth up and doun
The beautee of thise floryns newe and brightė.
'O Lord!' quod he, 'if so were that I myghtė
Have al this tresor to myself allonė,
Ther is no man that lyveth under the tronė
Of God that sholdė lyve so murye as I!'

And before too long, the Devil, our greatest enemy,
Suggested he buy some poison
So that he might dispose of his two mates;

Off he went, straight to the apothecary
And asked if he would be good enough to sell him
Some poison; he said it was to put down some rats.
Indeed there was a polecat trying to get at his chickens
And he wouldn't mind being rid of that too
And all the other vermin that was after his property.

The apothecary agreed, 'You can have some
Of this poison here, which, Gold help me,
Works almost instantly on any creature.'

No sooner had he got the poison than he ran
Into the next street to see a man
And borrowed three large bottles from him.
And he put the poison into two of them.
He kept the third clean for himself to drink out of.
You see he planned to work up a thirst that night
Carrying all the gold back to town.
So as soon as he had filled the three bottles with wine
This wretched villain made his way back to his two
    mates.

What more do I need to say?
The murder that the two devised

And attè laste the feend, oure enemý,
Putte in his thought that he sholde poyson beyè,
With which he myghtè sleen hise felawes tweyè;

And forth he gooth no lenger wolde he tarie,
Into the toun, unto a pothecarie,
And preydè hym that he hym woldè sellè
Som poyson, that he myghte hise rattès quellè;
And eek ther was a polcat in his hawè
That, as he seyde, hise capouns haddè yslawè,
And fayn he woldè wreke hym, if he myghtè,
On vermyn that destroyèd hym by nyghtè.

The pothecarie answérde, 'And thou shalt havè
A thyng that, also God my soulè savè,
In al this world ther is no crèatúrè
That ete or dronke hath of this confitúrè
Noght but the montance of a corn of whetè,
That he ne shal his lif anon forletè.'

This cursèd man hath in his hond yhent
This poysoun in a box, and sith he ran
Into the nextè strete unto a man,
And borwed of hym largè botels thre:
And in the two his poyson pourèd he,
The thriddè he keptè clenè for his drynkè;
For al the nyght he shoope hym for to swynkè
In cariynge of the gold out of that placè.
And whan this riotour with sory gracè
Haddè filled with wyn hise gretè botels thre,
To hise feláwes agayn repaireth he.

What nedeth it to sermone of it moorè?
For right as they haddè cast his deeth bifoorè,

Was carried out according to plan.
And when the deed was done, the ring leader said,
'Now let us drink and be merry
And when we're done, we'll bury his body.'
And with that he just happened
To pick up one of the poisoned bottles
And took a large swig, then offered it to his mate.
Within seconds they both lay dead.

**And so you see the three
Met Death at the old oak tree.**

Right so they han hym slayn, and that anon.
And whan that this was doon, thus spak that oon:
'Now lat us sitte and drynke, and make us merie,
And afterward we wol his body berie.'
And with that word it happèd hym, par cas,
To take the botel ther the poyson was,
And drank, and yaf his felawe drynke alsó,
For which anon they storven bothè two.

The Monkey's Paw

WITHOUT, THE NIGHT was cold and wet, but in the small parlour of Laburnum Villa the blinds were drawn and the fire burned brightly. Father and son were at chess.

'Hark at the wind,' said Mr White.

'I'm listening,' said the son, grimly surveying the board as he stretched out his hand. 'Check.'

'I should hardly think that he'd come tonight,' said his father, with his hand poised over the board.

'Mate,' replied the son.

'That's the worst of living so far out,' bawled Mr White, with sudden and unlooked-for violence; 'of all the beastly, slushy, out-of-the-way places to live in, this is the worst. Path's a bog, and road's a torrent. I don't know what people are thinking about. I suppose because only two houses in the road are let, they think it doesn't matter.'

'Never mind, dear,' said his wife, soothingly; 'perhaps you will win the next one.'

Mr White looked up sharply, just in time to intercept a knowing glance between mother and son. The words died away on his lips, and he hid a guilty grin in his thin grey beard.

'There he is,' said Herbert White, as the gate banged to loudly and heavy footsteps came towards the door.

The old man rose with hospitable haste, and opening the door, was heard condoling with the new arrival. The new arrival also condoled with himself, so that Mrs White said, 'Tut, Tut!' and coughed gently as her husband entered the room, followed by a tall, burly man, beady of eye and rubicund of visage.

'Sergeant-Major Morris,' he said, introducing him.

The sergeant-major shook hands, and taking the proffered seat by the fire, watched contentedly while his host got out whisky and tumblers and stood a small copper kettle on the fire.

At the third glass his eyes got brighter, and he began to talk, the little family circle regarding with eager interest this visitor from distant parts, as he squared his broad shoulders in the chair and spoke of wild scenes and doughty deeds; of wars and plagues and strange peoples.

'Twenty-one years of it,' said Mr White, nodding at his wife and son. 'When he went away he was a slip of a youth in the warehouse. Now look at him.'

'He don't look to have taken much harm,' said Mrs White politely.

'I'd like to go to India myself,' said the old man, 'just to look around a bit, you know.'

'Better where you are,' said the sergeant-major, shaking his head. He put down the empty glass, and, sighing softly, shook his head again.

'I should like to see those old temples and fakirs and jugglers,' said the old man. 'What was that you started telling me the other day about a monkey's paw or something, Morris?'

'Nothing,' said the soldier hastily. 'Leastways nothing worth hearing.'

'Monkey's paw?' said Mrs White curiously.

'Well, it's just a bit of what you might call magic, perhaps,' said the sergeant-major, offhandedly.

His three listeners leaned forward eagerly. The visitor absent-mindedly put his empty glass to his lips and then set it down again. His host filled it for him.

'To look at,' said the sergeant-major, fumbling in his pocket, 'it's just an ordinary little paw, dried to a mummy.'

He took something out of his pocket and proffered it. Mrs White drew back with a grimace, but her son, taking it, examined it curiously.

'And what is there special about it?' inquired Mr White as he took it from his son, and having examined it, placed it upon the table.

'It had a spell put on it by an old fakir,' said the sergeant-major, 'a very holy man. He wanted to show that fate ruled people's lives, and that those who interfered with it did so to their sorrow. He put a spell on it so that three separate men could each have three wishes from it.'

His manner was so impressive that his hearers were conscious that their light laughter jarred somewhat.

'Well, why don't you have three, sir?' said Herbert White, cleverly.

The soldier regarded him in the way that middle age is wont to regard presumptuous youth.

'I have,' he said quietly, and his blotchy face whitened.

'And did you really have the three wishes granted?' asked Mrs White.

'I did,' said the sergeant-major, and his glass tapped against his strong teeth.

'And has anybody else wished?' persisted the old lady.

'The first man had his three wishes. Yes,' was the reply. 'I don't know what the first two were, but the third was for death. That's how I got the paw.'

His tones were so grave that a hush fell upon the group.

'If you've had your three wishes, it's no good to you now, then, Morris,' said the old man at last. 'What do you keep it for?'

The soldier shook his head. 'Fancy, I suppose,' he said slowly. 'I did have some idea of selling it, but I don't think I will. It has caused enough mischief already. Besides, people won't buy. They think it's a fairy tale, some of them; and those who do think anything of it want to try it first and pay me afterwards.'

'If you could have another three wishes,' said the old man, eyeing him keenly, 'would you have them?'

'I don't know,' said the other. 'I don't know.'

He took the paw, and dangling it between his forefinger and thumb, suddenly threw it upon the fire. White, with a slight cry, stooped down and snatched it off.

'Better let it burn,' said the soldier solemnly.

'If you don't want it, Morris,' said the other, 'give it to me.'

'I won't,' said his friend doggedly. 'I threw it on the fire. If you keep it, don't blame me for what happens. Pitch it on the fire again, like a sensible man.'

The other shook his head and examined his new possession closely. 'How do you do it?' he inquired.

'Hold it up in your right hand and wish aloud,' said the sergeant-major, 'but I warn you of the consequences.'

'Sounds like *Arabian Nights*,' said Mrs White, as she rose and began to set the supper. 'Don't you think you might wish for four pairs of hands for me?'

Her husband drew the talisman from his pocket, and then all three burst into laughter as the sergeant-major, with a look of alarm on his face, caught him by the arm.

'If you must wish,' he said gruffly, 'wish for something sensible.'

Mr White dropped it back in his pocket, and placing chairs, motioned his friend to the table. In the business of supper the talisman was partly forgotten, and afterwards the three sat listening in an enthralled fashion to a second instalment of the soldier's adventures in India.

'If the tale about the monkey's paw is not more truthful than those he has been telling us,' said Herbert, as the door closed behind their guest, just in time to catch the last train, 'we shan't get much out of it.'

'Did you give him anything for it, father?' inquired Mrs White, regarding her husband closely.

'A trifle,' said he, colouring slightly. 'He didn't want it, but I made him take it. And he pressed me again to throw it away.'

'Likely,' said Herbert, with pretended horror. 'Why,

we're going to be rich, and famous and happy. Wish to be an Emperor, father, to begin with; then you can't be henpecked.'

He darted round the table, pursued by the maligned Mrs White.

Mr White took the paw from his pocket and eyed it dubiously.

'I don't know what to wish for, and that's a fact,' he said, slowly.

'It seems to me I've got all I want.'

'If you only cleared the house, you'd be quite happy, wouldn't you?' said Herbert, with his hand on his shoulder. 'Well, wish for two hundred pounds then; that'll just do it.'

His father, smiling shamefacedly at his own credulity, held up the talisman, as his son, with a solemn face, somewhat marred by a wink at his mother, sat down at the piano and struck a few impressive chords.

'I wish for two hundred pounds,' said the old man distinctly.

A fine crash from the piano greeted the words, interrupted by a shuddering cry from the old man. His wife and son ran towards him.

'It moved,' he cried, with a glance of disgust at the object as it lay on the floor.

'As I wished, it twisted in my hand like a snake.'

'Well, I don't see the money,' said his son, as he picked it up and placed it on the table, 'and I bet I never shall.'

'It must have been your fancy, father,' said his wife, regarding him anxiously.

He shook his head. 'Never mind, though; there's no harm done, but it gave me a shock all the same.'

They sat down by the fire again while the two men finished their pipes. Outside, the wind was higher than ever, and the old man started nervously at the sound of a door banging upstairs. A silence unusual and depressing settled upon all three, which lasted until the old couple arose to retire for the night.

'I expect you'll find the cash tied up in a big bag in the middle of your bed,' said Herbert, as he bade them good night, 'and something horrible squatting up on top of your wardrobe watching you as you pocket your ill-gotton gains.'

He sat alone in the darkness, gazing at the dying fire, and seeing faces in it. The last face was so horrible that he gazed at it in amazement. It got so vivid that, with a little uneasy laugh, he felt on the table for a glass containing a little water to throw over it. His hand grasped the monkey's paw, and with a little shiver he wiped his hand on his coat and went up to bed.

In the brightness of the wintry sun next morning as it streamed over the breakfast table, he laughed at his fears. There was an air of prosaic wholesomeness about the room which it had lacked on the previous night, and the dirty, shrivelled little paw was pitched on the sideboard with a carelessness which betokened no great belief in its virtues.

'I suppose all old soldiers are the same,' said Mrs White. 'The idea of our listening to such nonsense! How could wishes be granted in these days? And if they could, how could two hundred pounds hurt you, father?'

'Might drop on his head from the sky,' said the frivolous Herbert.

'Morris said the things happened so naturally,' said his father, 'that you might if you so wished attribute it to coincidence.'

'Well, don't break into the money before I come back,' said Herbert as he rose from the table. 'I'm afraid it'll turn you into a mean, avaricious man, and we shall have to disown you.'

His mother laughed, and following him to the door, watched him down the road; and returning to the breakfast table, was very merry at the expense of her husband's credulity. All of which did not prevent her from scurrying to the door at the postman's knock, nor prevent her from referring somewhat shortly to retired sergeant-majors of bibulous habits when she found that the post brought a tailor's bill.

'Herbert will have some more of his funny remarks, I expect, when he comes home,' she said, as they sat at dinner.

'I dare say,' said Mr White, pouring himself out some beer; 'but for all that, the thing moved in my hand; that I'll swear to.'

'You thought it did,' said the old lady soothingly.

'I say it did,' replied the other. 'There was no thought about it; I had just – What's the matter?'

His wife made no reply. She was watching the mysterious movements of a man outside, who, peering in an undecided fashion at the house, appeared to be trying to make up his mind to enter. In mental connexion with the two hundred pounds, she noticed that the stranger was well dressed, and wore a silk hat of glossy newness. Three times he paused at the gate, and then walked on again. The fourth time he stood with his hand upon it, and then with sudden resolution flung it open and walked up the path. Mrs White at the same moment placed her hands behind her, and hurriedly unfastening the strings of her apron, put that useful article of apparel beneath the cushion of her chair.

She brought the stranger, who seemed ill at ease, into the room. He gazed at her furtively, and listened in a preoccupied fashion as the old lady apologised for the appearance of the room, and her husband's coat, a garment which he usually reserved for the garden. She then waited as patiently as her sex would permit, for him to broach his business, but he was at first strangely silent.

'I – was asked to call,' he said at last, and stooped and picked a piece of cotton from his trousers. 'I come from "Maw and Meggins".'

The old lady started. 'Is anything the matter?' she asked breathlessly. 'Has anything happened to Herbert? What is it?'

Her husband interposed. 'There, there, mother,' he said hastily. 'Sit down and don't jump to conclusions. You've not brought bad news, I'm sure, sir;' and he eyed the other wistfully.

'I'm sorry –' began the visitor.

'Is he hurt?' demanded the mother wildly.

The visitor bowed in assent. 'Badly hurt,' he said quietly, 'but he is not in any pain.'

'Oh, thank God!' said the old woman, clasping her hands. 'Thank God for that! Thank –'

She broke off suddenly as the sinister meaning of the assurance dawned upon her, and she saw the awful confirmation of her fears in the other's averted face. She caught her breath, and turning to her slower-witted husband, laid her trembling old hand upon his. There was a long silence.

'He was caught in the machinery,' said the visitor at length in a low voice.

'Caught in the machinery,' repeated Mr White in a dazed fashion, 'yes.'

He sat staring blankly out at the window, and taking his wife's hand between his own, pressed it as he had been wont to do in their old courting days nearly forty years before.

'He was the only one left to us,' he said, turning gently to the visitor. 'It is hard.'

The other coughed, and rising, walked slowly to the window. 'The firm wished me to convey their sincere sympathy with you in your great loss,' he said without looking around. 'I beg that you will understand I am only their servant and merely obeying orders.'

There was no reply; the old woman's face was white, her eyes staring, and her breath inaudible; and on the husband's face was a look such as his friend the sergeant might have carried into his first action.

'I was to say that Maw and Meggins disclaim all responsibility,' continued the other. 'They admit no liability at all, but in consideration of your son's services, they wish to present you with a certain sum as compensation.'

Mr White dropped his wife's hand, and rising to his feet, gazed with a look of horror at his visitor. His dry lips shaped the words, 'How much?'

'Two hundred pounds,' was the answer.

Unconscious of his wife's shriek, the old man smiled faintly, put out his hands like a sightless man, and dropped, a senseless heap, to the floor.

In the huge new cemetery, some miles distant, the old people buried their dead, and came back to a house steeped in shadow and silence. It was all over so quickly that at first they could hardly realise it, and remained in a state of expectation as though of something else to happen – something else which was to lighten this load, too heavy for old hearts to bear.

But the days passed, and expectation gave place to resignation – the hopeless resignation of the old, sometimes miscalled apathy. Sometimes, they hardly exchanged a word, for now they had nothing to talk about, and their days were long to weariness.

It was about a week after, that the old man, waking suddenly in the night, stretched out his hand and found himself alone. The room was in darkness, and the sound of subdued weeping came from the window. He raised himself in bed and listened.

'Come back,' he said, tenderly. 'You will be cold.'

'It is colder for my son,' said the old woman, and wept afresh.

The sound of her sobs died away on his ears. The bed was warm, and his eyes heavy with sleep. He dozed fitfully and then slept until a sudden wild cry from his wife awoke him with a start.

'*The paw*!' she cried wildly. 'The monkey's paw!'

He started up in alarm. 'Where? Where is it? What's the matter?'

She came stumbling across the room towards him. 'I want it,' she said quietly. 'You've not destroyed it?'

'It's in the parlour, on the bracket,' he replied, marvelling. Why?'

She cried and laughed together, and bending over, kissed his cheek.

'I only just thought of it,' she said, hysterically. 'Why didn't I think of it before? Why didn't you think of it?'

'Think of what?' he questioned.

'The other two wishes,' she replied, rapidly. 'We've only had one.'

'Was not that enough?' he demanded fiercely.

'No,' she cried triumphantly; 'we'll have one more. Go down and get it quickly, and wish our boy alive again.'

The man sat up in bed and flung the bedclothes from his quaking limbs. 'Good God, you are mad!' he cried aghast.

'Get it,' she panted, 'get it quickly, and wish – Oh, my boy, my boy!'

Her husband struck a match and lit the candle. 'Get back to bed,' he said unsteadily. 'You don't know what you are saying.'

'We had the first wish granted,' said the old woman, feverishly; 'why not the second?'

'A coincidence,' stammered the old man.

'Go and get it and wish,' cried his wife, quivering with excitement.

The old man turned and regarded her, and his voice shook. 'He has been dead ten days, and besides he – I would not tell you else, but – I could only recognise him by his clothing. If he was too terrible for you to see then, how now?'

'Bring him back,' cried the old woman, and dragged him towards the door. 'Do you think I fear the child I have nursed?'

He went down in the darkness, and felt his way to the parlour, and then to the mantelpiece. The talisman was in its place, and a horrible fear that the unspoken wish might bring his mutilated son before him ere he could escape from the room seized upon him, and he caught his breath as he found that the had lost the direction of the door. His brow cold with sweat, he felt his way round the table, and groped along the wall until he found himself in the small passage with the unwholesome thing in his hand.

Even his wife's face seemed changed as he entered the room. It was white and expectant, and to his fears seemed to have an unnatural look upon it. He was afraid of her.

'*Wish*,' she cried in a strong voice.

'It is foolish and wicked,' he faltered.

'*Wish*!' repeated his wife.

He raised his hand. 'I wish my son alive again.'

The talisman fell to the floor, and he regarded it fearfully. Then he sank trembling into a chair as the old woman, with burning eyes, walked to the window and raised the blind.

He sat until he was chilled with the cold, glancing occasionally at the figure of the old woman peering through the window. The candle-end, which had burned below the rim of the china candlestick, was throwing pulsating shadows on the ceiling and walls, until, with a flicker larger than the rest, it expired. The old man, with an unspeakable sense of relief at the failure of the talisman, crept back to his bed, and a minute or two afterwards the old woman came silently and apathetically beside him.

Neither spoke, but lay silently listening to the ticking of the clock. A stair creaked, and a squeaky mouse scurried noisily through the wall. The darkness was oppressive, and after lying for some time, screwing up his courage, he took the box of matches, and striking one, went downstairs for a candle.

At the foot of the stairs the match went out, and he paused to strike another; and at the same moment a knock, so quiet and stealthy as to be scarcely audible, sounded on the front door.

The matches fell from his hand and spilled in the passage. He stood motionless, his breath suspended until the knock was repeated. Then he turned and fled swiftly back to his room, and closed the door behind him. A third knock sounded through the house.

'*What's that?*' cried the old woman, starting up.

'A rat,' said the old man in shaking tones, '- a rat. It passed me on the stairs.'

His wife sat up in bed listening. A loud knock resounded through the house.

'It's Herbert!' she screamed. 'It's Herbert!'

She ran to the door, but her husband was before her, and catching her by the arm, held her tightly.

'What are you going to do?' he whispered hoarsely.

'It's my boy; it's Herbert!' she cried, struggling mechanically. 'I forgot it was two miles away. What are you holding me for? Let go. I must open the door.'

'For God's sake don't let it in,' cried the old man, trembling.

'You're afraid of your own son,' she cried, struggling. 'Let me go. I'm coming, Herbert; I'm coming.'

There was another knock, and another. The old woman with a sudden wrench broke free and ran from the room. Her husband followed to the landing, and called after her appealingly as she hurried downstairs. He heard the chain rattle back and the bottom bolt drawn slowly and stiffly from the socket. Then the old woman's voice, strained and panting.

'The bolt,' she cried loudly. 'Come down. I can't reach it.'

But her husband was on his hands and knees groping wildly on the floor in search of the paw. If he could only find it before the thing outside got in. A perfect fusillade of knocks reverberated through the house, and he heard the scraping of a chair as his wife put it down in the passage against the door. He heard the creaking of the bolt as it came slowly back, and at the same moment he found the monkey's paw, and frantically breathed his third and last wish.

The knocking ceased suddenly, although the echoes of it were still in the house. He heard the chair drawn back, and the door opened. A cold wind rushed up the staircase, and a long loud wail of disappointment and misery from his wife gave him the courage to run down to her side, and then to the gate beyond. The street lamp flickering opposite shone on a quiet and deserted road.

A New England Nun

IT WAS LATE in the afternoon, and the light was waning. There was a difference in the look of tree shadows out in the yard. Somewhere in the distance cows were lowing and a little bell was tinkling; now and then a farm-wagon tilted by, and the dust flew; some blue-shirted laborers with shovels over their shoulders plodded past; little swarms of flies were dancing up and down before the people's faces in the soft air. There seemed to be a gentle stir arising over everything for the mere sake of subsidence – a very premonition of rest and hush and night.

This soft diurnal commotion was over Louisa Ellis also. She had been peacefully sewing at her sitting-room window all the afternoon. Now she quilted her needle carefully into her work, which she folded precisely, and laid it in a basket with her thimble and thread and scissors.

Lousia tied a green apron round her waist, and got

out a flat straw hat with a green ribbon. Then she went into the garden with a little blue crockery bowl, to pick some currants for her tea. After the currants were picked she sat on the back doorstep and stemmed them, collecting the stems carefully in her apron, and afterward throwing them into the hen-coop. She looked sharply at the grass beside the step to see if any had fallen there.

Louisa was slow and still in her movements; it took her a long time to prepare her tea; but when ready it was set forth with as much grace as if she had been a veritable guest to her own self. The little square table stood exactly in the centre of the kitchen, and was covered with a starched linen cloth whose border pattern of flowers glistened. Louisa had a damask napkin on her tea-tray, where were arranged a cut-glass tumbler full of teaspoons, a silver cream-pitcher, a china sugar-bowl, and one pink china cup and saucer. Louisa used china every day – something which none of her neighbors did. They whispered about it among themselves. Their daily tables were laid with common crockery, their sets of best china stayed in the parlor closet, and Louisa Ellis was no richer nor better bred than they. Still she would use the china. She had for her supper a glass dish full of sugared currants, a plate of little cakes, and one of light white biscuits. Also a leaf or two of lettuce, which she cut daintily. Louisa was very fond of lettuce, which she raised to perfection in her little garden. She ate quite heartily, though in a delicate, pecking way; it seemed almost surprising that any considerable bulk of the food should vanish.

After tea she filled a plate with nicely baked thin corn-cakes, and carried them out into the backyard.

'Caesar!' she called. 'Caesar! Caesar!'

There was a little rush, and the clank of a chain, and a large yellow-and-white dog appeared at the door of his tiny hut, which was half hidden among the tall grasses and flowers. Louisa patted him and gave him the corn-cakes. Then she returned to the house and washed the tea-things, polishing the china carefully. The twilight had deepened; the chorus of the frogs floated in at the open window wonderfully loud and shrill, and once in a while a long sharp drone from a tree-toad pierced it. Louisa took off her green gingham apron, disclosing a shorter one of pink-and-white print. She lighted her lamp, and sat down again with her sewing.

In about half an hour Joe Dagget came. She heard his heavy step on the walk, and rose and took off her pink-and-white apron. Under that was still another – white linen with a little cambric edging on the bottom; that was Louisa's company apron: She never wore it without her calico sewing-apron over it unless she had a guest. She had barely folded the pink-and-white one with methodical haste and laid it in a table-drawer when the door opened and Joe Dagget entered.

He seemed to fill up the whole room. A little yellow canary that had been asleep in his green cage at the south window woke up and fluttered wildly, beating his little yellow wings against the wires. He always did so when Joe Dagget came into the room.

'Good-evening,' said Louisa. She extended her hand with a kind of solemn cordiality.

'Good-evening, Louisa,' returned the man, in a loud voice.

She placed a chair for him, and they sat facing each other, with the table between them. He sat bolt-upright, toeing out his heavy feet squarely, glancing with a good-humored uneasiness around the room. She sat gently erect, folding her slender hands in her white-linen lap.

'Been a pleasant day,' remarked Dagget.

'Real pleasant,' Louisa assented, softly. 'Have you been haying?' she asked, after a little while.

'Yes, I've been haying all day, down in the ten-acre lot. Pretty hot work.'

'It must be.'

'Yes, it's pretty hot work in the sun.'

'Is your mother well today?'

'Yes, mother's pretty well.'

'I supposed Lily Dyer's with her now?'

Dagget colored. 'Yes, she's with her,' he answered, slowly.

He was not very young, but there was a boyish look about his large face. Louisa was not quite as old as he, her face was fairer and smoother, but she gave people the impression of being older.

'I suppose she's a good deal of help to your mother,' she said, further.

'I guess she is; I don't know how mother'd get along without her,' said Dagget, with a sort of embarrassed warmth.

'She looks like a real capable girl. She's pretty-looking too,' remarked Louisa.

'Yes, she is pretty fair-looking.'

Presently Dagget began fingering the books on the table. There was a square red autograph album, and a Young Lady's Gift-Book which had belonged to Louisa's mother. He took them up one after the other and opened them; then laid them down again, the album on the Gift-Book.

Louisa kept eying them with mild uneasiness. Finally she rose and changed the position of the books, putting the album underneath. That was the way they had been arranged in the first place.

Dagget gave an awkward little laugh. 'Now what difference did it make which book was on top?' said he.

Louisa looked at him with a deprecating smile. 'I always keep them that way,' murmured she.

'You do beat everything,' said Dagget, trying to laugh again. His large face was flushed.

He remained about an hour longer, then rose to take leave. Going out, he stumbled over a rug, and, trying to recover himself, hit Louisa's work-basket on the table, and knocked it on the floor.

He looked at Louisa, then at the rolling spools; he ducked himself awkwardly toward them, but she stopped him. 'Never mind,' said she; 'I'll pick them up after you're gone.'

She spoke with a mild stiffness. Either she was a little disturbed, or his nervousness affected her, and made her seem constrained in her effort to reassure him.

When Joe Dagget was outside he drew in the sweet evening air with a sigh, and felt much as an innocent and perfectly well-intentioned bear might after his exit from a china shop.

Louisa, on her part, felt much as the kind-hearted, long-suffering owner of the china shop might have done after the exit of the bear.

She tied on the pink, then the green apron, picked up all the scattered treasures and replaced them in her work-basket, and straightened the rug. Then she set the lamp on the floor, and began sharply examining the carpet. She even rubbed her fingers over it, and looked at them.

'He's tracked in a good deal of dust,' she murmured. 'I thought he must have.'

Louisa got a dustpan and brush, and swept Joe Dagget's track carefully.

He came twice a week to see Louisa Ellis, and every time, sitting there in her delicately sweet room, he felt as if surrounded by a hedge of lace. He was afraid to stir lest he should put a clumsy foot or hand through the fairy web, and he had always the consciousness that Louisa was watching fearfully lest he should.

Still the lace and Louisa commanded perforce his perfect respect and patience and loyalty. They were to be married in a month, after a singular courtship which had lasted for a matter of fifteen years. For fourteen out of the fifteen years the two had not once seen each other, and they had seldom exchanged letters. Joe had been all those years in Australia, where he had gone to make his fortune, and where he had stayed until he made it. He would have stayed fifty years if it had taken so long, and come home feeble and tottering, or never come home at all, to marry Louisa.

But the fortune had been made in the fourteen years, and he had come home now to marry the woman who had been patiently and unquestioningly waiting for him all that time.

Shortly after they were engaged he had announced to Louisa his determination to strike out into new fields, and secure a competency before they should be married.

'It won't be for long,' poor Joe had said, huskily; but it was for fourteen years.

In that length of time much had happened. Louisa's mother and brother had died, and she was all alone in the world. But greatest happening of all – a subtle happening which both were too simple to understand – Louisa's feet had turned into a path, smooth maybe under a calm, serene sky, but so straight and unswerving that it could only meet a check at her grave, and so narrow that there was no room for anyone at her side.

Louisa's first emotion when Joe Dagget came home (he had not apprised her of his coming) was consternation, although she would not admit it to herself, and he never dreamed of it. Fifteen years ago she had been in love with him – at least she considered herself to be. She had listened with calm docility to her mother's views upon the subject. Her mother was remarkable for her cool sense and sweet, even temperament. She talked wisely to her daughter when Joe Dagget presented himself, and Louisa accepted him with no hesitation. He was the first lover she had ever had.

She had been faithful to him all these years. She had never dreamed of the possibility of marrying anyone else. Her life, especially for the last seven years, had been full of a pleasant peace, she had never felt discontented nor impatient over her lover's absence; still she had always looked forward to his return and their marriage as the inevitable conclusion of things. However, she had fallen into a way of placing it so far in the future that it was almost equal to placing it over the boundaries of another life.

When Joe came she had been expecting him, and

expecting to be married for fourteen years, but she was as much surprised and taken aback as if she had never thought of it.

Joe's consternation came later. He eyed Louisa with an instant confirmation of his old admiration. She had changed but little. She still kept her pretty manner and soft grace, and was, he considered, every whit as attractive as ever. As for himself, his stint was done; he had turned his face away from fortune-seeking, and the old winds of romance whistled as loud and sweet as ever through his ears. All the song which he had been wont to hear in them was Louisa; he had for a long time a loyal belief that he heard it still, but finally it seemed to him that although the winds sang always that one song, it had another name. But for Louisa the wind had never more than murmured; now it had gone down, and everything was still. She listened for a little while with half-wistful attention; then she turned quietly away and went to work on her wedding-clothes.

Joe had made some extensive and quite magnificent alterations in his house. It was the old homestead; the newly married couple would live there, for Joe could not desert his mother, who refused to leave her old home. So Louisa must leave hers. Every morning, rising and going about among her neat maidenly possessions, she felt as one looking her last upon the faces of dear friends.

Louisa had almost the enthusiasm of an artist over the mere order and cleanliness of her solitary home. She had throbs of genuine triumph at the sight of the window-panes which she had polished until they shone like jewels. She gloated gently over her orderly bureau-drawers, with their exquisitely folded contents redolent with lavender and sweet clover and very purity. Could she be sure of the endurance of even this? She had visions, so startling that she half repudiated them as indelicate, of coarse masculine belongings strewn about in endless litter; of dust and disorder arising necessarily from a coarse masculine presence in the midst of all this delicate harmony.

Among her forebodings of disturbance, not the least was with regard to Caesar. Caesar was a veritable hermit of a dog. For the greater part of his life he had dwelt in his secluded hut, shut out from the society of his kind and all innocent canine joys. Never had Caesar since his early youth watched at a woodchuck's hole; never had he known the delights of a stray bone at a neighbor's kitchen door. And it was all on account of a sin committed when hardly out of his puppyhood.

Old Caesar seldom lifted up his voice in a growl or a bark; he was fat and sleepy; there were yellow rings which looked like spectacles around his dim old eyes; but there was a neighbor who bore on his hand the imprint of several of Caesar's sharp, white, youthful teeth, and for that he had lived at the end of the chain, all alone in a little hut, for fourteen years. The neighbor, who was choleric and smarting with pain of his wound, had demanded either Caesar's death or complete ostracism. So Louisa's brother, to whom the dog had belonged, had built him his little kennel and tied him up. It was now fourteen years since, in a flood of youthful spirits, he had inflicted that memorable bite, and with the exception of short excursions, always at the end of the chain, under the strict guardianship of his master or Louisa, the old dog had remained a close prisoner. He was regarded by all the children in the village and by many adults as a very monster of ferocity. Joe Dagget, however, with his good-humored sense and shrewdness, saw him as he was. He strode valiantly up to him and patted him on the head, in spite of Louisa's soft clamor of warning, and even attempted to set him loose. Louisa grew so alarmed that he desisted, but kept announcing his opinon in the matter quite forcibly at intervals. 'There ain't a better-natured dog in town,' he would say, 'and it's downright cruel to keep him tied up there. Some day I'm going to take him out.'

Louisa had very little hope that he would not, one of these days, when their interests and possessions should be more completely fused in one. She pictured to herself Caesar on the rampage through the quiet and unguarded village. She saw innocent children bleeding in his path. She was herself very fond of the old dog, because he had belonged to her dead brother, and he was always very gentle with her; still she had great faith in his ferocity. She always warned people not to go too near him. She fed him on corn-mush and cakes, and never fired his dangerous temper with heating and sanguinary diet of flesh and bones. Louisa looked at the old dog munching his simple fare, and thought of her approaching marriage and trembled. Joe Dagget had been fond of her and working for her all these years. It was not for her, whatever came to pass, to prove untrue and break his heart. She put the exquisite little stitches into her wedding-garments, and the time went on until it was only a week before her wedding-day. It was a Tuesday evening, and the wedding was to be a week from Wednesday.

There was a full moon that night. About nine o'clock

Louisa strolled down the road a little way. There were harvest-fields on either hand, bordered by low stone walls. Luxuriant clumps of bushes grew beside the wall, and trees – wild cherry and old apple trees – at intervals. Presently Louisa sat down on the wall and looked about her with mildly sorrowful reflectiveness.

She was just thinking of rising, when she heard footsteps and low voices, and remained quiet. It was a lonely place, and she felt a little timid. She thought she would keep still in the shadow and let the persons, whoever they might be, pass her.

But just before they reached her the voices ceased, and the footsteps. She understood that their owners had also found seats upon the stone wall. She was wondering if she could not steal away unobserved, when the voice broke the stillness. It was Joe Dagget's. She sat still and listened.

The voice was announced by a loud sigh, which was as familiar as itself. 'Well,' said Dagget, 'you've made up your mind, then, I suppose?'

'Yes,' returned another voice; 'I'm going day after tomorrow.'

'That's Lily Dyer,' thought Louisa to herself. The voice embodied itself in her mind. She saw a girl tall and full-figured, with a firm, fair face, looking fairer and firmer in the moonlight, her strong yellow hair braided in a close knot. A girl full of a calm rustic strength and bloom, with a masterful way which might have beseemed a princess. Lily Dyer was a favorite with the village folk; she had just the qualities to arouse the admiration. She was good and handsome and smart. Louisa had often heard her praises sounded.

'Well,' said Joe Dagget, 'I ain't got a word to say.'

'I don't know what you could say,' returned Lily Dyer.

'Not a word to say,' repeated Joe, drawing out the words heavily. Then there was a silence. 'I ain't sorry,' he began at last, 'that that happened yesterday – that we kind of let on how we felt to each other. I guess it's just as well we knew. Of course, I can't do anything any different. I'm going right on an' get married next week. I ain't going back on a woman that's waited for me fourteen years, an' break her heart.'

'If you should jilt her tomorrow, I wouldn't have you,' spoke up the girl, with sudden vehemence.

'Well, I ain't going to give you the chance,' said he; 'but I don't believe you would, either.'

'You'd see I wouldn't. Honor's honor, an' right's right. An' I'd never think anything of any man that went against 'em for me or any other girl; you'd find that out, Joe Dagget.'

'Well, you'll find out fast enough that I ain't going against 'em for you or any other girl,' returned he. Their voices sounded almost as if they were angry with each other. Louisa was listening eagerly.

'I'm sorry you feel as if you must go away,' said Joe, 'but I don't know but it's best.'

'Of course it's best. I hope you and I have got common-sense.'

'Well, I suppose you're right.' Suddenly Joe's voice got an undertone of tenderness. 'Say, Lily,' said he, 'I'll get along well enough myself, but I can't bear to think – You don't suppose you're going to fret much over it?'

'I guess you'll find out I sha'n't fret much over a married man.'

'Well, I hope you won't – I hope you won't, Lily. God knows I do. And – I hope – one of these days – you'll – come across somebody else –'

'I don't see any reason why I shouldn't.' Suddenly her tone changed. She spoke in a sweet, clear voice, so loud that she could have been heard across the street. 'No, Joe Dagget,' said she, 'I'll never marry any other man as long as I live. I've got good sense, an' I ain't going to break my heart nor make a fool of myself; but I'm never going to be married, you can be sure of that. I ain't that sort of girl to feel this way twice.'

Louisa heard an exclamation and a soft commotion behind the bushes; then Lily spoke again – the voice sounded as if she had risen. 'This must be put a stop to,' said she. 'We've stayed here long enough. I'm going home.'

Louisa sat there in a daze, listening to their retreating steps. After a while she got up and slunk softly home herself. The next day she did her housework methodically; that was as much a matter of course as breathing; but she did not sew on her wedding-clothes. She sat at her window and meditated. In the evening Joe came. Louisa Ellis had never known that she had any diplomacy in her, but when she came to look for it that night she found it, although meek of its kind, among her little feminine weapons. Even now she could hardly believe that she had heard aright, and that she would not do Joe a terrible injury should she break her troth-plight. She wanted to sound him without betraying too soon her own inclinations in the matter. She did it successfully, and they finally came to an understanding; but it was a difficult thing, for he was as afraid of betraying himself as she.

She never mentioned Lily Dyer. She simply said that while she had no cause of complaint against him, she had lived so long in one way that she shrank from making a change.

'Well, I never shrank, Louisa,' said Dagget. 'I'm going to be honest enough to say that I think maybe it's better this way; but if you'd wanted to keep on, I'd have stuck on you till my dying day. I hope you know that.'

'Yes, I do,' said she.

That night she and Joe parted more tenderly than they had done for a long time. Standing in the door, holding each other's hands, a last great wave of regretful memory swept over them.

'Well, this ain't the way we've thought it was all going to end, is it, Louisa?' said Joe.

She shook her head. There was a little quiver on her placid face.

'You let me know if there's ever anything I can do for you,' said he. 'I ain't ever going to forget you, Louisa.' Then he kissed her, and went down the path. Louisa, all alone by herself that night, wept a little, she hardly knew why; but the next morning, on waking, she felt like a queen who, after fearing lest her domain be wrested away from her, sees it firmly insured in her possession.

Now the tall weeds and grasses might cluster around Caesar's little hermit hut, the snow might fall on its roof year in and year out, but he never would go on a rampage through the unguarded village. Louisa could sew linen seams, and distil roses, and dust and polish and fold away in lavender, as long as she listed. That afternoon she sat with her needlework at the window, and felt fairly steeped in peace. Lily Dyer, tall and erect and blooming, went past; but she felt no qualm. If Louisa Ellis had sold her birthright she did not know it, the taste of the pottage was so delicious, and had been her sole satisfaction for so long. Serenity and placid narrowness had become to her as the birthright itself. She gazed ahead through a long reach of future days strung together like pearls in a rosary, every one like the others, and all smooth and flawless and innocent, and her heart went up in thankfulness. Outside was the fervid summer afternoon; the air was filled with the sounds of the busy harvest of men and birds and bees; there were halloos, metallic clattering, sweet calls, and long hummings. Louisa sat, prayerfully numbering her days, like an uncloistered nun.

The Necklace

SHE WAS ONE of those pretty and charming girls, who had been born by an unlucky twist of fate into a lower middle-class family. She had no dowry, no hope of inheriting any money, and it was unlikely that she would ever meet a man of wealth and social position who might appreciate her, love her and marry her. And so she allowed herself to be married to a junior clerk in the Ministry of Public Instruction.

She did not have enough money for expensive clothes or jewellery, so she dressed simply. She was unhappy, feeling that she was destined for better things in life. A woman should have no social class; her place in society should depend upon her beauty, her grace and her charm. If she possessed a natural sense of refinement, instinctive good taste and an agile mind, a woman from quite an ordinary family should be able to compete with the grandest lady in the land.

She fretted constantly, feeling that she had been born for all the luxuries and finer things of life. She resented her humble surroundings; the bare walls, the shabby furniture, the ugly fabrics. She was tormented and angered by these things, though another woman of her class would not have even noticed them. Even the sight of her little Breton maid doing the housework aroused in her feelings of hopeless longing for things that could never be. She dreamt of hushed ante-chambers, the oriental hangings lit by tall, bronze candelabra, and of two imposing footmen in knee-britches, slumbering in great armchairs by the drowsy heat of the stove. She dreamt of magnificent drawing rooms, furnished with ancient silks, fine antiques and priceless ornaments, and of chic, perfumed boudoirs, ideal for afternoon conversation with one's closest friends; or with those fashionable gentlemen that every woman longs to entertain.

When she and her husband sat down to eat at the round dining table, and he took the lid off the soup tureen, exclaiming delightedly, 'Ah, beef stew, my favourite,' she would look at the three-day-old cloth and dream of elegant dinner parties. She would picture the gleaming silver on the table, and imagine tapestries adorning the walls with mythical scenes. She would dream of eating delicacies served on exquisite porcelain, and of accepting whispered compliments with an enigmatic smile, whilst she savoured the pink flesh of a trout or the plump wing of a pullet.

She had no elegant clothes, no jewels, nothing. Yet she desired nothing else. She felt that she was meant for a life of fashion. She longed to be attractive, to be envied, to be surrounded by admirers.

She had a rich friend from her school days, but she stopped going to visit her. It was so painful to return from her friend's fine home to her own poor apartment, that she would fall into a deep depression and cry for days afterwards.

Then, one evening, her husband came home proudly holding a large envelope. She tore it open and took out a printed card on which were the words, 'The Minister of Public Instruction and Madame Georges Ramponneau request the pleasure of the company of Monsieur and Madame Loisel at the Ministry on Monday the 18th of January.'

Instead of the delight which her husband had expected, she threw the invitation onto the table and muttered peevishly, 'And what do you expect me to do about it?'

'But, my dear, I thought you'd be happy. You never get the chance to go out, and this is a real occasion. I went to a lot of trouble to get this invitation. They're really hard to come by. Everyone wants one and they don't give many to junior clerks. Anybody who *is* anybody will be there.'

She glanced at him irritably and snapped, 'And just what do you think I am going to wear to this ball?'

This was not something that he had even thought of.

He stammered, 'Well, the dress you go to the threatre in. It seems very nice to me ...'

He lapsed into a stunned silence, lost for words, when he saw that his wife was crying. Two large tears were running slowly down her face.

'But ... but what's wrong, what's wrong with you?'

With a supreme effort, she overcame her emotions,

and drying her tears, she replied, calmly, 'Nothing. It's simply that I have nothing to wear and so I cannot possibly go to this ball. It would be better if you gave the invitation to a colleague whose wife is better dressed than I am.'

Her husband was distressed by this, and replied, 'Look, Mathilde, how much would a suitable dress cost; something simple that you could wear again afterwards?'

She thought it over for a few seconds, taking into account the amount of money they had, and calculating the sum she could ask for without shocking her cautious husband into dismissing the idea out of hand.

At last she replied, hesitantly, 'I'm not exactly sure, but I think that I could manage with four hundred francs.'

He paled slightly, because that was the exact sum that he was saving to buy a gun, so that he could go lark-shooting with his friends, on Sundays during the Summer.

In spite of this, he said, 'All right. I'll give you four hundred francs. But try to buy yourself a really beautiful dress.'

As the day of the ball drew nearer, Madame Loisel still seemed downcast and anxious, although her new dress was ready.

'What's wrong? You've been in a strange mood for three days,' her husband asked her one evening.

'I haven't got a single piece of jewellery; not one stone to wear. It would almost be better not to go to this party at all.'

'Why not wear fresh flowers. They are particularly

fashionable this season. For ten francs you could buy two or three lovely roses.'

She remained unconvinced.

'No, there is nothing more humiliating than to be poor when you are surrounded by rich women.'

Suddenly, her husband exclaimed, 'How silly you are! Go and see your friend Madame Forestier and ask her if you can borrow some of her jewellery! You know her well enough for that.'

She cried out in delight. 'You're right! Why didn't I think of it myself?'

The next day, she went to see her friend and told her about the problem. Madame Forestier went to a glass-fronted cabinet and produced a large jewellery case. Opening it, she said, 'Choose what you like, my dear.'

First, Madame Loisel saw some bracelets and a pearl necklace, then she saw a Venetian cross, delicately worked in gold and precious stones. She tried the jewels on in front of the mirror and hesitated, unable either to take them off, or to put them back in the box.

All the time she kept asking, 'Have you anything else?'

'Of course, of course. Just carry on looking. I don't know exactly what you want.'

Suddenly, she came across a superb diamond necklace in a black satin case, and her heart began to beat wildly. As she picked it up, her hands shook. She put it on over her high-necked dress and stared at herself in ecstasy.

'Could you lend me this? Just this and nothing else?' she asked, hesitantly.

'Yes, of course.'

She threw her arms round her friend's neck, kissing

her delightedly, then rushed home with her prize.

The day of the party arrived. Madame Loisel was the the Belle of the Ball. She was the prettiest woman there; elegant and graceful; smiling and vivacious. She attracted the gaze of all the men, who wanted to know who she was and who tried to get themselves introduced to her. All the top ministry officials wanted to dance with her. Even the Minister himself noticed her.

She danced with abandon, carried away on a cloud of happiness, where nothing mattered to her except the sweetness of the triumph that she had longed for.

It was four in the morning when she left the dance floor. Since midnight, her husband had been asleep in the adjoining room, with three other gentlemen whose wives were still enjoying themselves.

As they prepared to go home, Monsieur Loisel draped round her shoulders the cloak she wore every day. The elegance of her ball gown emphasised its dowdiness, and she was suddenly brought down to earth. All she wanted was to leave as quickly as possible, so that she would not be seen by the other women, who were wrapping themselves in rich furs.

Loisel called, 'Wait a moment. It's cold outside. I'll get a carriage.'

She wouldn't listen to him and ran down the steps. Once they were in the street, they found that all the carriages were taken, so they started to hail the passing coachmen, looking for one that was free.

Shivering and disheartened, they made their way towards the River Seine. Eventually, they found an ancient cab down by the riverside. It was one of those ramshackle vehicles that you only see in Paris at night, as if they were ashamed to reveal their shabbiness in the cold light of day.

It took them to the door of their house in the Rue des Martyrs, and they dejectedly climbed the stairs. For her, it was all over. His only thought was that he had to be at the office by ten o'clock. She took off her cloak and stood once more in front of the mirror to see herself in all her glory. But suddenly she cried out. Her neck was bare. The diamond necklace had gone!

Her husband, already half undressed, asked, 'What's the matter?'

She turned to him in horror.

'The necklace. It's gone!'

'What do you mean? How? It's not possible!'

They searched everywhere. In the folds of her dress, in the pleats of her cloak, in her pockets, but they found nothing.

'Are you sure you had it when you left the ball?' he asked.

'Yes, I remember touching it as we were leaving.'

'But we would have heard it if it had fallen off in the street. You must have lost it in the carriage.'

'Yes, that must be what happened. Can you remember the number?'

'No, did you notice it?'

'No.'

They stared at each other in dismay. Finally, Loisel got dressed again.

'I'll go back over the route where we walked and see if I can find it.'

He went out. Still in her evening dress, she sank in a chair, her mind and body numb with shock. Her husband returned at about seven o'clock in the morning. He had found nothing.

He went to the police station, to the newspapers, to the cab companies; everywhere that might have given them a glimmer of hope. She waited at home all day in the same state of shock, contemplating the terrible disaster. Loisel returned at about seven that evening, his face pale and drawn. There was no trace.

'You must write to your friend and tell her that you have broken the clasp and that you are having it mended. That will give us the time to think of something.'

After a week had passed, they had lost all hope of ever finding the necklace. Loisel, who now looked five years older, said, 'We'll just have to think of a way to replace it.'

So the next day, they took the case that it had come in, and went to the jewellers whose name was inside the lid. He consulted his books.

'I'm afraid that I did not sell this necklace. I must have only supplied the case.

Sick with anxiety, they went from jeweller to jeweller, searching for a necklace like the one that had been lost, trying hard to remember exactly what it had looked like.

Eventually, in a small shop in the Palais Royal, they found a diamond necklace which seemed to be identical to the one they had lost. It was worth 40,000 francs, but the jeweller said he would let them have it for 36,000.

They persuaded him to keep it for them for three days, on condition that he would buy it from them for 34,000 francs if they should find the original before the end of February. Loisel had 18,000 francs which his father had left him and he would just have to borrow the rest.

He borrowed a thousand francs from one person, five hundred from another; five louis here, three louis there. He wrote IOUs, borrowed money at outrageous rates of interest, dealing with all kind of unscrupulous money-lenders. He mortgaged the rest of his life, signing documents without knowing if he would ever be able to honour the debts. He was panic-stricken at the prospect of the physical hardship, mental torture and black despair that he faced in the future, but finally, he went to collect the necklace, putting the 36,000 francs on the counter.

When Madame Loisel returned the necklace, Madame Forestier said coldly, 'You should have brought it back sooner. I might have needed it.'

She didn't open the case as her friend had feared she might. What if she had noticed the change? What would she have thought? What would she have said? Would she have thought that Madame Loisel had stolen it?

Madame Loisel came to know the life of the very poor. She resigned herself bravely to the inevitable. The terrible debt had to be paid and she would pay it. They got rid of the maid and moved to cheaper lodgings, renting an attic room.

She did all the heavy housework and the dirty kitchen jobs. She washed all the dishes, breaking her pink finger nails on the crockery and greasy saucepans. She washed the dirty linen, the shirts and the dish-cloths, hanging them out to dry on the line. Every morning, she took the rubbish down to the street and carried the water back up the stairs, stopping to catch her breath on each landing. She dressed like a working woman, and with her basket on her arm, she bargained with the greengrocer, the grocer and the butcher, braving their insults in order to eke out, penny by penny, her pitiful housekeeping money.

Every month she had to pay off some debts, whilst others were renewed to buy more time. In the evenings, her husband kept the books for a tradesman, and often at night, he did copywriting for five sous a page.

And so their lives continued for ten years. At the end of that time, they had paid everything back; everything, including all the interest that had accrued.

Madame Loisel looked like an old woman now. She had become strong, hard and coarse, like the women you find in the homes of the poor. She would scrub the floors, talking at the top of her voice, heedless of her uncombed hair, her disordered skirts and her red hands. But sometimes, when her husband was at the office, she would sit at the window and dream of that evening which now seemed to belong to another time; of that ball, when she had been so beautiful and so much admired.

What would her life have been like if she had not lost that necklace? Who could say? Who could know? How strange life is. How suddenly things change! It takes so little to turn happiness into despair.

One Sunday, she had gone for a stroll in the Champs Elysee to get away from her everyday cares and worries. Suddenly, she caught sight of a woman and child walking along together. It was Madame Forestier, still young, still beautiful, still attractive.

Madame Loisel was overcome with emotion. Should she go and speak to her? Yes, of course, now that she'd paid off the debt, she'd tell her everything. Why not?

She went up to her.

'Hello Jeanne.'

The other woman showed no sign of recognition, but looked astonished that this common female should address her by her first name.

She stammered, 'But Madame ... I don't know ... you must have mistaken me for someone else.'

'No. I am Mathilde Loisel.'

Her friend uttered a cry.

'Oh, my poor Mathilde. How you have changed!'

'Yes. Life has been hard since I last saw you. I've had my fair share of suffering ... and it's all because of you.'

'Because of me ... what do you mean?'

'Do you remember lending me that diamond necklace to go to the party at the Ministry?'

'Yes ... what about it?'

'Well, I lost it!'

'What? But you gave it back to me.'

'I gave you back another one, exactly like it, and it's taken ten years to pay for it. I'm sure you will understand that it wasn't easy for us, because we had nothing. Anyway, it's done now, and I'm glad it's over.'

Madame Forestier had stopped in her tracks.

'Are you telling me that you bought a diamond necklace to replace the one I lent you?'

'Yes, and you didn't notice, did you? They were exactly the same.'

She smiled with simple pride and joy.

Deeply moved, Madame Forestier took both her hands.

'Oh, my poor Mathilde. My necklace was paste. It was worth five hundred francs at most ...'

The Gift of the Magi

ONE DOLLAR AND eighty-seven cents. That was all. And sixty cents of it was in pennies. Pennies saved one and two at a time by bulldozing the grocer and the vegetable man and the butcher. Three times Della counted it. One dollar and eighty-seven cents. And the next day would be Christmas.

There was clearly nothing to do but flop down on the shabby little couch and howl. So Della did it.

Whilst the mistress of the home is gradually subsiding from the first state to the second, take a look at the home. A furnished flat at eight dollars per week.

In the vestibule below was a letter-box into which no letter would go, and an electric button from which no mortal finger could coax a ring. Also there was a card bearing the name 'Mr James Dillingham Young.'

The 'Dillingham' had been flung to the breeze during

a former period of prosperity when its possessor was being paid thirty dollars per week. Now, when the income was shrunk to twenty dollars, the letters of 'Dillingham' looked blurred, as though they were thinking seriously of contracting to a modest and unassuming D. But whenever, Mr James Dillingham Young came home and reached his flat above he was called 'Jim' and greatly hugged by Mrs James Dillingham Young, already introduced to you as Della. Which is all very good.

Della finished her cry and attended to her cheeks with a powder puff. She stood by the window and looked out dully at a grey cat walking a grey fence in a grey back yard. Tomorrow would be Christmas Day, and she had only $1.87 with which to buy Jim a present. She had been saving every penny she could for months, with this result. Twenty dollars a week doesn't go far. Expenses had been greater than she had calculated. They always are. Only $1.87 to buy a present for Jim. Her Jim. Many a happy hour she had spent planning for something nice for him. Something fine and rare and sterling – something just a little bit near to being worthy of the honour of being owned by Jim.

There was a pier glass between the windows of the room. Perhaps you have seen a pier glass in an eight-dollar flat. A very thin and very agile person may, by observing his reflection in a rapid sequence of longitudinal strips, obtain a fairly accurate conception of his looks. Della, being slender, had mastered the art.

Suddenly she whirled from the window and stood before the glass. Her eyes were shining brilliantly, but her face had lost its colour within twenty seconds.

Rapidly she pulled down her hair and let if fall to its full length.

Now, there were two possessions of the James Dillingham Youngs in which they both took a mighty pride. One was Jim's gold watch that had been his father's and his grandfather's. The other was Della's hair. Had the Queen of Sheba lived in the flat across the airshaft, Della would have let her hair hang out the window some day to dry just to depreciate Her Majesty's jewels and gifts. Had King Solomon been the janitor, with all his treasures piled up in the basement, Jim would have pulled out his watch every time he passed, just to see him pluck at his beard from envy.

So now Della's beautiful hair fell about her, rippling and shining like a cascade of brown waters. She did it up again nervously and quickly. Once she faltered for a minute while a tear splashed on the worn red carpet.

On went her old brown jacket; on went her old brown hat. With a whirl of skirts and with the brilliant sparkle still in her eyes, she fluttered out the door and down the stairs to the street.

Where she stopped the sign read: 'Mme. Sofronie. Hair Goods of All Kinds.' One flight up Della ran, and collected herself, panting. Madame, large, too white, chilly, hardly looked the 'Sofronie'.

'Will you buy my hair?' asked Della.

'I buy hair,' said Madame. 'Take yer hat off and let's have a sight at the looks of it.'

Down rippled the brown cascade.

'Twenty dollars,' said Madame, lifting the mass with a practised hand.

'Give it to me quick,' said Della.

Oh, and the next two hours tripped on rosy wings. Forget the hashed metaphor. She was ransacking the stores for Jim's present.

She found it at last. It surely had been made for Jim and no one else. There was no other like it in any of the stores, and she had turned all of them inside out. It was a platinum watch-chain, simple and chaste in design, properly proclaiming its value by substance alone and not by ornamentation – as all good things should do. It was even worthy of The Watch. As soon as she saw it she knew that it must be Jim's. It was like him. Quietness and value – the description applied to both. Twenty-one dollars they took from her for it, and she hurried home with the eighty-seven cents. With that chain on his watch Jim might be properly anxious about the time in any company. Grand as the watch was, he sometimes looked at it on the sly on account of the shabby old leather strap that he used in place of a proper gold chain.

When Della reached home her intoxication gave way a little to prudence and reason. She got out her curling-irons and lighted the gas and went to work repairing the ravages made by generosity added to love. Which is always a tremendous task, dear friends – a mammoth task.

Within forty minutes her head was covered with tiny close-lying curls that made her look wonderfully like a truant schoolboy. She looked at her reflection in the mirror long, carefully, and critically.

'If Jim doesn't kill me,' she said to herself, 'before he takes a second look at me, he'll say I look like a Coney Island chorus girl. But what could I do – oh! what could I do with a dollar and eighty-seven cents?'

At seven o'clock the coffee was made and the frying-pan was in the back of the stove, hot and ready to cook the chops.

Jim was never late. Della doubled the watch chain in her hand and sat on the corner of the table near the door that he always entered. Then she heard his step on the stair away down on the first flight, and she turned white for just a moment. She had a habit of saying little silent prayers about the simplest everyday things, and now she whispered: 'Please, God, make him think I am still pretty.'

The door opened and Jim stepped in and closed it. He looked thin and very serious. Poor fellow, he was only twenty-two – and had to be burdened with a family! He needed a new overcoat and he was without gloves.

Jim stepped inside the door, as immovable as a setter at the scent of quail. His eyes were fixed upon Della, and there was an expression in them that she could not read, and it terrified her. It was not anger, nor surprise, nor disapproval, nor horror, nor any of the sentiments that she had been prepared for. He simply stared at her fixedly with that peculiar expression on his face.

Della wriggled off the table and went for him.

'Jim, darling,' she cried, 'don't look at me that way. I had my hair cut off and sold it because I couldn't have lived through Christmas without giving you a present. It'll grow out again – you won't mind, will you? I just had to do it. My hair grows awfully fast. Say "Merry Christmas!" Jim, and let's be happy. You don't know what a nice – what a beautiful, nice gift I've got for you.'

'You've cut off your hair?' asked Jim, laboriously, as

if he had not arrived at that patent fact yet even after the hardest mental labour.

'Cut it off and sold it,' said Della. 'Don't you like me just as well, anyhow? I'm me without my hair, ain't I?'

Jim looked about the room curiously.

'You say your hair is gone?' he said, with an air almost of idiocy.

'You needn't look for it,' said Della. 'It's sold, I tell you – sold and gone, too. It's Christmas Eve, boy. Be good to me, for it went for you. Maybe the hairs of my head were numbered,' she went on with a sudden serious sweetness, 'but nobody could ever count my love for you. Shall I put the chops on, Jim?'

Out of his trance Jim seemed to quickly wake. He enfolded his Della. Eight dollars a week or a million a year – what is the difference? A mathematician or a wit would give you the wrong answer. The Magi brought valuable gifts, but that was not among them. This dark assertion will be illuminated later on.

Jim drew a package from his overcoat pocket and threw it upon the table.

'Don't make any mistake, Dell,' he said, 'about me. I don't think there's anything in the way of a haircut or a shave or a shampoo that could make me like my girl any less. But if you'll unwrap that package you may see why you had me going awhile at first.'

White fingers and nimble tore at the string and paper. And then an ecstatic scream of joy; and then, alas! a quick feminine change to hysterical tears and wails, necessitating the immediate employment of all the comforting power of the lord of the flat.

For there lay The Combs – the set of combs that Della

had worshipped for long in a Broadway window. Beautiful combs, pure tortoise shell, with jewelled rims – just the shade to wear in the beautiful vanished hair. They were expensive combs, she knew, and her heart had simply craved and yearned over them without the least hope of possession. And now they were hers, but the tresses that should have adorned the coveted adornments were gone.

But she hugged them to her bosom, and at length she was able to look up with dim eyes and a smile and say: 'My hair grows so fast, Jim!'

And the Della leaped up like a little singed cat and cried, 'Oh, oh!'

Jim had not yet seen his beautiful present. She held it out to him eagerly upon her open palm. The dull precious metal seemed to flash with a reflection of her ardent spirit.

'Isn't it a dandy, Jim? I hunted all over town to find it. You'll have to look at the time a hundred times a day now. Give me your watch. I want to see how it looks on it.'

Instead of obeying, Jim tumbled down on the couch and put his hands under the back of his head and smiled.

'Dell,' said he, 'let's put our Christmas presents away and keep 'em a while. They're too nice to use just at present. I sold the watch to get the money to buy your combs. And now suppose you put the chops on.'

The Magi, as you know, were wise men – wonderfully wise men – who brought gifts to the Babe in the manger. They invented the art of giving Christmas presents. Being wise, their gifts were no doubt wise ones, possibly bearing the privilege of exchange in case of duplication. And here I have lamely related to you the uneventful chronicle of two foolish children in a flat who most unwisely sacrificed for each other the greatest treasures of their house. But in a last word to the wise of these days let it be said that of all who give gifts these two were the wisest. Of all who give and receive gifts, such as they are the wisest. Everywhere they are the wisest. They are the Magi.

Glossary: reading the text

1 *Tinderbox*   an old-fashioned lighter.

13 *Jinn*   another name for a genie.

15 *vassal*   a slave.

42 *cubits*   ancient measurement; one cubit was the length of the forearm.

   span   measurement from thumb to little finger.

   shekels   old measurement of weight.

43 *greaves*   armour to protect the shins.

46 *countenance*   face.

84 *Pardoner*   in the Middle Ages a Pardoner would pardon people's sins. He was also supposed to teach people to live their lives better so that they could get to heaven.

98 *apothecary*   a chemist.

104 *fakir*   a religious man.

108 *prosaic*   things were back to normal.

109 *credulity*   believing things easily.

   bibulous   alcoholic.

116 *fusillade*   like shots going off rapidly.

125 *repudiated*   refused to admit that she had such thoughts.

128 *vehemence*   with great feeling, passionately.

129 *troth-plight*   promise of marriage.

133 *boudoir*   a private room for a woman.

143 *Magi*   the three Wise Men who brought gifts to the baby Jesus.

vestibule   a small entrance hall.

149 *coveted*   the things she wanted more than anything.

Study programme

In this section you will find assignments on the individual stories as well as ones which allow you to compare and contrast stories.

Classic fairy tales

'The Tinderbox'

1. Write an article for a newspaper which reveals the 'rags to riches' story of the young soldier.

'The Magic Ring'

2. The Jinn serves both masters in this story. Imagine that you are the Jinn and write diary entries about the events in the story. Try to capture his attitude to his two masters.

Comparing the stories

3. The best way to write about two or more stories, novels, plays or poems is to compare them by theme or idea. Compile a list of things which your texts have in common; then choose the two or three main common features, comparing them one by one and drawing conclusions about them as you go.

Taking a comparison of '**The Tinderbox**' and '**The Magic Ring**' as an example:

- both have a character who comes into possession of a gift with magic powers
- magic is used in both stories
- there is an evil character
- there are parents
- there is also a princess
- there are marriages.

When you have made your list, select the two or three headings that you can write about in most depth. Take them one by one and at the end of each section make your own comments about what you think the author is trying to say to us through the themes and ideas.

Winners

'The Creation of Man'

☐ What do you think of this version of Man's beginning? Compare it with other versions of Man's creation which you can research via the school library.

When you have completed the research, you can use this as the basis for a discussion on the creation of the universe and its life forms.

'From Tiger to Anansi'

2 Write Anansi's pamphlet, giving advice on how to outwit snakes. It should include diagrams to help the reader follow Anansi's plans. It should also contain hints on how to outwit other large and dangerous enemies.

'David and Goliath'

3 There are two versions of this story: a modern translation and a translation done for King James I in 1611. Look at the two stories and note down the ways in which the modern version differs from the older one. Use the following headings:

- different words
- different word orders
- the way the story is told
- details.

Comparing the stories

4 All three stories revolve around one central character outwitting others. They are also concerned with the victims.

- What is it about the three central characters which makes them winners in a struggle?
- What is it about their victims which causes them to lose?

Learning a lesson

'The Conceited Man'

1. Write two reports on the progress of Li Chao up to the time when he leaves the monk's academy:

   - one from the point of view of Li Chao

   - one from the point of view of the monk.

'The Selfish Giant'

2. This story is in two halves. In the first half, darkness, anger and bad weather are most important; in the second, good weather, happiness and light prevail. Rewrite this story, setting it in the present day and choosing a real life character instead of the giant. Try to keep the elements of gloom in the first half of your story and the elements of lightness in the second.

'Tseng and the Holy Man'

3. Research the character of Scrooge in **A Christmas Carol** by Charles Dickens. When you have done this, write down as many as you can of the things that the characters of Scrooge and Tseng have in common.

4. Many films have been made about Scrooge, both with real actors and in cartoon form. Which medium would you choose for this story: cartoon or actors? What sections of the story do you think would be the most interesting to film?

Comparing the stories

5. In each of the three stories there is a character who starts off bad and changes his ways. Discuss:

- the characters and their faults
- what happens in each story to make the character change
- which story you think gets its message across most effectively.

Russian gypsy stories

1. Adapt either '**Gypsies Who All But Cheated Themselves**' or '**The Gypsy Who Did Not Keep His Word**' for the radio. Write it in playscript form and add sound effects where necessary.

Comparing the stories

2. Draw up two columns on a sheet of A4 headed SIMILARITIES and DIFFERENCES. When you have done this, write two or three paragraphs on the similarities; then do the same with the differences. In a final paragraph try to decide what you think is the moral or message of each story.

Norwegian stories – death by drowning

1. Imagine you are the vicar in either '**The Father**' or

'**The Fisherman**'. Write your diary entries for the days when you have had meetings with either Tor or Isak.

Comparing the stories

2 These stories have many features in common and they offer a good opportunity for comparative writing. For example, both stories include the following:

- a vicar who has to deal with one of his parishioners – each vicar has a very different approach
- relationships within a family – father/son, brother/brother
- death by drowning, and the effect it has upon a person
- a character who changes his ways
- references to family values.

Compare the ways these themes are treated in each story.

Losers

'The Pardoner's Tale'

1 A Pardoner's job was to help people get to heaven. He would pardon them their sins and try to teach them to live their lives in a better way. This story is

like a sermon or parable: it was designed to show what happened to people who sinned.

The tale manages to include each of the SEVEN DEADLY SINS: Avarice, Lust, Sloth, Pride, Envy, Gluttony and Anger. If you are not sure of the meaning of any of these words, look them up in the dictionary.

Now read through the translation of the tale and make a note of all the things the three louts do wrong, and see if you can find the occasions when they commit one of the Seven Deadly Sins.

Look across at the original text (printed in italics), and see if you can find the exact lines for each of the sins. Notice which words are the same, which words are similar and which are quite different.

Finally, write an essay entitled 'Sins and Sinners', in which you discuss the the crimes of the three louts. Try to include a quotation for each of the important sections – use the original text when quoting.

2 Write a present-day version of '**The Pardoner's Tale**'.

'The Monkey's Paw'

3 Look at the first two pages of the story and note down any words and phrases which give the impression that serious and dark events are going to happen in it.

4. Write a sequel to this story, entitled 'The Monkey's Paw 2'.

Comparing both stories

5. These stories provide good subjects for comparison although they were written at very different times. Both are warnings about dabbling with things that go against nature. Both involve:

   - characters who are tempted
   - a character who tempts the others
   - tragic and horrific events
   - money and greed
   - a strong moral message.

   Explore similarities and differences in the way these themes are dealt with in the two stories.

Relationships

'A New England Nun'

1. Write a letter from Louisa to an 'Agony Aunt' just after she has overheard Joe's and Lily's conversation.

2. This story is an example of nineteenth-century American English. What do you notice about the language used – the spellings, the phrasing and any unusual words?

'The Necklace'

3 Write Mathilde's letter to her sister, in which she explains the ups and downs of her life.

'The Gift of the Magi'

4 Discuss the following issues:

- Which of the two characters, Della or Jim, made the greater sacrifice?
- What do you think is the moral to this story?

Comparing the stories

5 Each of these three stories involves a strong female character. Write about the pressures each of them faces. Do you think that the outcome in each story would have been different if it were set in modern times?

Further assignments – themes for comparison

In the assignments you have completed so far, you have been comparing the stories according to their groupings in the book. You can of course compare any of the stories as long as they have some common elements. The list of headings below will help you find common themes and ideas in the stories:

1. **Money** Does money, the lack of it or the desire for it, play a part in any story?

2. **Travel** Do characters move to different locations? What effect does it have on them?

3. **Time** How long does each story last? Draw a time line to find out.

4. **Animals** Do they play a significant part in the story?

5. **Objects** Are there any important objects mentioned in the story? Do these objects influence what happens in any way?

6. **Strangers** Are there any lone, unusual characters who play a small but significant part in the story?

7. **Unexpected meetings** Are there any important locations used for these meetings? Do they give the story a particular atmosphere?

8. **Moral** Is there a strong message or moral in the story?

9. **Relationships** Are there any new relationships formed in the story? Are any relationships changed or broken?

10. **Mood** What is the story like to read? Is it sad, humorous, unusual? How does it make you feel?

11 Narrative style   How is the story told? Look at the language used – is it complicated or is it straightforward? Was it designed to reach a particular audience?

12 Turning point   Is there a significant moment in the story when its direction changes.

Longman Literature

Series editor: Roy Blatchford

Novels

Jane Austen   **Pride and Prejudice**   0 582 07720 6
Nina Bawden   **The Real Plato Jones**   0 582 29254 9
Charlotte Brontë   **Jane Eyre**   0 582 07719 2
Emily Brontë   **Wuthering Heights**   0 582 07782 6
Anita Brookner   **Hotel du Lac**   0 582 25406 X
Marjorie Darke   **A Question of Courage**   0 582 25395 0
Charles Dickens   **A Christmas Carol**   0 582 23664 9
                 Great Expectations   0 582 07783 4
                 Oliver Twist   0 582 28729 4
George Eliot   **Silas Marner**   0 582 23662 2
Josephine Feeney   **My Family and Other Natural Disasters**   0 582 29262 X
Anne Fine   **The Book of the Banshee**   0 582 29258 1
            Flour Babies   0 582 29259 X
            Goggle-Eyes   0 582 29260 3
            Madame Doubtfire   0 582 29261 1
            A Pack of Liars   0 582 29257 3
            Step by Wicked Step   0 582 29251 4
F Scott Fitzgerald   **The Great Gatsby**   0 582 06023 0
                    Tender is the Night   0 582 09716 9
Nadine Gordimer   **July's People**   0 582 06011 7
Graham Greene   **The Captain and the Enemy**   0 582 06024 9
Thomas Hardy   **Far from the Madding Crowd**   0 582 07788 5
               The Mayor of Casterbridge   0 582 22586 8
               Tess of the d'Urbervilles   0 582 09715 0
Susan Hill   **The Mist in the Mirror**   0 582 25399 3
Lesley Howarth   **MapHead**   0 582 29255 7
Aldous Huxley   **Brave New World**   0 582 06016 8
Robin Jenkins   **The Cone-Gatherers**   0 582 06017 6
Doris Lessing   **The Fifth Child**   0 582 06021 4
Joan Lindsay   **Picnic at Hanging Rock**   0 582 08174 2
Bernard Mac Laverty   **Lamb**   0 582 06557 7
Jan Mark   **The Hillingdon Fox**   0 582 25985 1
Dalene Matthee   **Fiela's Child**   0 582 28732 4
Brian Moore   **Lies of Silence**   0 582 08170 X
Beverley Naidoo   **Journey to Jo'burg**   0 582 25402 7
George Orwell   **Animal Farm**   0 582 06010 9
Alan Paton   **Cry, the Beloved Country**   0 582 07787 7
Ruth Prawer Jhabvala   **Heat and Dust**   0 582 25398 5
Paul Scott   **Staying On**   0 582 07718 4
Catherine Sefton   **Along a Lonely Road**   0 582 29256 5
Robert Swindells   **Daz 4 Zoe**   0 582 30243 9
Anne Tyler   **A Slipping-Down Life**   0 582 29247 6
Edith Wharton   **Ethan Frome**   0 582 30244 7
Virginia Woolf   **To the Lighthouse**   0 582 09714 2

Other titles in the Longman Literature series are listed on pages ii and 165.

Longman Literature Shakespeare
Series editor: Roy Blatchford

Other titles in the Longman Literature series are listed on pages ii and 164.

Addison Wesley Longman Limited
Edinburgh Gate
Harlow
Essex CM20 2JE, England
and Associated Companies throughout the world.

Editorial material © Addison Wesley Longman Limited 1997

This educational edition first published 1997
Second impression 1997

Editorial material set in 12/14 point Gill Sans
Produced by Longman Singapore Publishers (Pte) Ltd
Printed in Singapore

ISBN 0 582 29253 0

The publisher's policy is to use paper manufactured from sustainable
forests.

Consultant: Geoff Barton